DEDICATION

For B.G., who never gave up on me

"Owning our story can be hard but not nearly as difficult as spending our lives running from it. Embracing our vulnerabilities is risky but not nearly as dangerous as giving up on love and belonging and joy—the experiences that make us the most vulnerable. Only when we are brave enough to explore the darkness will we discover the infinite power of our light."

- Brene Brown

TABLE OF CONTENTS

ACKNOWLEDGEMENTS

Every day I start with gratitude. It opens me up for miracles.

Therefore, it is the best place to begin this book.

First and foremost, I want to thank the two men in my life who have held the space so that I could create this book.

For my soul partner and husband:

You are the Yang to my Yin and the water to soothe my worries. I asked the universe to bring me the best partner and God sent you. Thank you for being on this journey with me and for making my life better and easier. I am deeply grateful for your shoulders to lean on, your hugs, your kisses, and your unconditional love for me exactly as I am.

For my beloved father:

You taught me the courage to never give up, to hold my head high and look fear in the eye and ROAR. You were a model of unshakable confidence and always in constant pursuit of knowledge. You passed your curiosity and hunger for information on to me. Your legacy allows me to dedicate myself full time to this pursuit and to seek out and learn from the greatest teachers.

Many other people played an important role on this journey and for whom I am deeply grateful.

To C and K, thank you for teaching me how to love without conditions.

To Innocent and the children of the Good Hope School, thank you for giving me a bigger purpose in life.

To my grandmother and mother, thank you for instilling in me a love for books and reading.

To my grandfather, thank you for always encouraging my creativity.

To all my spiritual teachers, thank you for guiding me.

Moreover, I would also like to thank my dear friends and Beta-Readers for their support and love along the way: Priscilla, Sandra, Natalie, Mari, Bella, Jackie, Natasha, Carrie, Trish, Dominique, Sevecen, Cheryl, Gloria, Yolanda, Angela, Anna Maria, Kelly, Phyllis. And to Carol and Deva Vani, thank you for holding a nurturing space.

Thank you to all the wonderful friends and family members around the globe who hosted me in their homes, and to the strangers and guardian angels who helped me in times of need.

Finally, thank you to my editor Coral Coons, book designer Danielle Cantin, and writer Jacqui Letran, for helping me see this project all the way through to fruition.

Last, but definitely not least, thank you Meg, for giving me the impetus to become to best version of myself.

Thank you ALL for birthing this book with me.

By believing in miracles, we create them together.

FOREWORD

Every blade of grass has an angel that bends over it and whispers, "Grow! Grow!"- Talmud

I started writing this book in September 2017, two weeks before my fiftieth birthday. I chose to channel my pain from a traumatic experience into creating something useful and beautiful. On the cover, you see a serene woman in a meditative pose, high atop a mountain. That image was selected with great care.

In every great story, there is a hero/heroine who is faced with some seemingly insurmountable obstacle. There are monsters to slay and a magnificent reward waiting at the end. This story is no different.

I, like most people, have faced many struggles, fallen many times, and experienced loss, pain, and disappointment. What makes my story different than others, perhaps, is how I chose to confront those obstacles. I just kept coming back, getting up, and moving forward, like the Ever-Ready bunny.

This is an autobiography of my life and my travels, but more than that, it is a do-it-yourself manual. In it, I have included the greatest lessons I have learned, the books I have read, the spiritual practices I have studied, and the steps I took to persevere.

What you get out of this book will depend entirely on how much you put into it. I have given you the tools. Use them. Dive into them. And keep putting one foot in front of the other until you reach your goal.

The stories are not chronological because life is messy, not orderly. Curve-balls catch us by surprise, and the only way to prepare for them is through practice.

Happiness is not a destination, as you will see. It is an inside journey. The greatest demon to conquer lies within our own minds—our fears, insecurities, and doubts. Once the inner battle is won, the path will clear and miracles will manifest. That woman on the cover is metaphor for my life. To find inner peace and lasting happiness, I had to do the work. You too must climb your own mountain.

I invite you to read each chapter more than once, especially the ones you find challenging. Read them alone or in a group. Start a dialogue with a friend or start a book club or study group. Get an accountability partner to do the steps together.

Human nature is to constantly seek the comfort zone. However, if you want a different result, you must take a different path.

I hope that this book inspires you the way so many books have inspired me. I hope it motivates you to grow, thrive, and prosper.

Now, let us embark on an adventure around the world. Pack your bags, get your passport ready, and let's take the leap together!

CHAPTER 1

Uganda

LESSON:

Just Do It!

"It's never too late to be whoever you want to be"
-F. Scott Fitzgerald

The year was 2009. I was teaching a class to the international students at UC San Diego. During the break time, I checked my cell phone and saw a missed call from my best friend's sister. I listened to her shaky voice message that started out, "Hi, Mica, this is Grace. I am sorry to say that Meg is gone." I could tell from the tone of her voice that she meant gone as in dead.

My knees buckled, and I fell to the floor. Some of my students saw me fall and came over to help me. I was on the floor, sobbing, wailing, tears running down my face, in a complete state of shock. My friend, whom I had just seen just a few days before, looking fit, happy, and beautiful, was gone. I had no warning. No chance to say goodbye.

My students picked me up and, together with a fellow teacher, carried me into the lounge, where I continued to bawl profusely. It was my first experience with a sudden death to a person close to me. I was utterly heartbroken.

I spent several weeks grieving. One of my friends who had experienced loss at a young age advised me to choose the quality that Meg embodied which I most admired and emulate that quality.

What was the quality I admired the most in my friend? She was the best mother I knew.

At the time, I was forty-one, single, and had no children. So, I asked myself, "How can I become a great mother like my friend?" Many people would have given up on becoming a mother at forty-one. But not me.

I believe in miracles. I asked myself, "If I want to be a mother, where are there children who need me?"

One month later, while attending a Landmark Leadership Seminar, I met a new friend, Jeanne, who was working on a project to help raise money for a school for orphans in Uganda. I had been wanting to do more philanthropic work, so I committed to helping her raise money. As I learned more about the school, my intuition kept giving me a very strong nudge saying, "JUST GO TO AFRICA!"

So, I got my visa and vaccinations, bought a plane ticket, contacted the family that ran the school, packed my bag, and flew alone for the very first time to Africa. That trip changed my life. Even though I was afraid to go to a strange place alone, I had faith and trust that the universe would continue to guide me. In other words, I felt the fear and did it anyway.

The journey was arduous. It took several days, flying overnight from the U.S. to Paris, to Ethiopia, to Uganda, then cross-country overnight on a rickety old bus packed to the gills with chickens, people, and packages. I had not slept the whole journey. I arrived exhausted and excited at dawn at the Good Hope School in Kabale, Uganda, located in the misty hills near the border of Rwanda. I collapsed on the bed and fell asleep immediately.

When I awoke, there were two hundred children waiting to greet me. They were so overjoyed to meet their new "Mama Mica" from America. We sang, danced, played, and learned from each other for three weeks. My broken heart was quickly mended and grew back stronger than before. From that day on, I became the official Mama Mica to the children of the Good Hope School. They gave me an African name, Mugisha, which means "gift".

They believed that I was a gift to them. But in truth, being with those children was one of the best gifts I have ever received. Doing charitable acts always makes me feel better. When we give to others, we give to ourselves. I could explain more about how it felt to be there in Africa with those kids, but it is better to watch for yourself. I made a YouTube video while teaching affirmations of success to the children. It was the first time that they had ever heard the message "You are POWERFUL!" My wish is by the time you finish reading this book, you will understand that you are powerful too.

Link: *https://youtu.be/5elGX8cdBDo*

So, as you can see, by acting as if I were a "mother", I became one. My lesson here is to JUST BE who you want to be.

CHOOSE to go for it and follow your dream. The universe WILL conspire to help you. Just keep taking the next step. And the next one. And the next one.

Miracles are created that way.

SIDE-NOTE

The Miraclecatcher Foundation, which I created in 2009, has contributed over twenty-five thousand US dollars to build homes and schools in Uganda, Kenya, Mexico, Burma, and the United States. Hundreds of children have received books, school supplies, clothing, seeds, and food.

To watch the video of me teaching at the Good Hope School, go to: **https://youtu.be/5elGX8cdBDo**

For more information on The Good Hope School, go to **www. goodhopeschool.net**

For more information on the Miraclecatcher Foundation, go to **www.facebook.com/ TheMiraclecatcherFoundation**

Reflection Questions

1. Where is somewhere you would like to go but have never gone to because of fear, money, or time constraints? What are some ways you could accomplish this goal? Who do you know who has already accomplished this goal? For some extra tips on how to travel for free, read my blog at **www.miraclecatcher.com.**

2. When have you given up on a dream? Look at your life and find one area where you used to have passion but don't anymore. How could you jump-start that dream? Did you play an instrument? Did you write stories? Did you do a sport that you loved? Why did you stop? Did someone tell you to stop? Why did you believe that person?

3. Do you want to be a parent? Are you waiting for the right person? The right time? The right income? What are some ways you could contribute to the children who are already in your life? Or the children in your neighborhood?

4. What are some ways you could get involved in a charity or community project? Is there something happening in the world which interests you or upsets you? What could you do to help?

_____

_____

_____

_____

Get Into Action

Choose one thing you want to do but haven't done yet because of time, money, or fear. Do some research. Ask five people who have already accomplished this goal for advice on how to make it happen. If you need money, create a crowd-funding campaign or seek a grant or scholarship. Make a SMART goal plan (Google: What is a SMART goal?) to accomplish your goal within one year. Carpe Diem. Seize the day!

Book Recommendation: *The Success Principles* by Jack Canfield has an excellent resource section on finding a mentor and goal setting.

CHAPTER 2

Italy

LESSON:

Celebrate Your Uniqueness

I went to Italy to meet my relatives for the first time in 1982. Italy had just won the World Cup Soccer Championship, and there were people celebrating, honking horns, yelling, hooting, kissing, dancing, and cheering in the streets. It was my first visit to the "motherland".

I have more than twenty-five direct cousins in Italy. Most of my father's family still lives there. And even though my father was born and raised in Italy, I did not learn Italian as a child. The first time I went, I only knew a few words of Italian, and I was both completely amazed and shocked at the same time.

I went when I was a sophomore in high school. Where I grew up, in Southern California, it was "cool" to be blonde and tan. I remember being teased for being too loud, too chatty, and having too much dark, thick, wavy hair. In the South of Italy, everywhere I went, there were people who looked just like me, talked like me, and sounded like me. It was the first time in my life that I felt like I had found my "tribe". Even if I couldn't understand exactly what they were saying, I could feel their expressiveness, their passion, their feistiness!

For some of you reading this, it is normal to look around and see a very homogenous culture, but for some of you, it is not. This chapter is for those who feel that they are somehow different from the "norm." Whatever your differences are, be they physical, racial, sexual, political or religious, being different from everyone else is a challenge, especially in our younger formative years.

No doubt, most of you reading this got teased for something in school or even bullied. I got bullied for being different. One of my favorite quotes is from Dr. Seuss, who said, "Why fit in when you were born to stand out?"

My spiritual practice has taught me that we create tests for ourselves to grow. I look back now at those girls who teased me or bullied me, and here is what I see. I have compassion for them because I know that most bullies are bullied in their home by one or more parents, that people who feel the need to criticize others are usually toughest on themselves, and that many of those bullies grew up to become victims of their own negative energy.

I am happy to be "unique" now. It was my own passion and

outspokenness which led me on all these adventures. It is my freedom of self-expression that gave me the courage to write this book. It is my dark, thick hair, which is still healthy and strong at fifty-plus. All of those things which set me apart were gifts in disguise.

When I lived in Italy, from 1990 to 1993, I learned to fully embrace my Italian-ness. When I returned to the U.S., people said how much I had changed. It was not just my hairstyle and clothing that had changed; it was my attitude as well. I had embraced my own beauty. Even if I am not tall and blonde, I am beautiful in my own way. No, I don't mean that in an arrogant way. I mean it in a healthy self-esteem way.

Nowadays, fortunately, there are different standards of beauty, and hopefully, this trend will continue to evolve to include all races and body types.

Walk down the cobblestone streets in Florence and Rome, and you will see beauty; it is everywhere. The art, the fashion, the architecture, the cars – Italy is a place which revels in beauty. Some foreign women feel uncomfortable there because the men stop and stare when a woman walks by. I say, bring it on! Let it in. Let yourself be appreciated. I am powerful, and I am a woman. We can be both.

Italian painters Tiziano and Botticelli worshipped the female body full of curves. They did not ask women to starve themselves to be loved.

I am grateful for my Italian skin, my Italian hair, and my Italian curves. I want to live in a world where all women feel beautiful, not in a grey world where everyone looks and talks the same. What is unique about you? Your true gifts are there. Don't let anyone steal your light.

Reflection Questions:

1. What are some of the things you like about your body? List ten.

2. Which country are your ancestors from? Which physical traits did you inherit from them? Have you been to that country? What did you like about it?

3. What are some attributes you have been teased about? Do those traits serve you now? What are some ways those attributes have made you stronger or better?

4. Have you internalized other people's criticism? Do you judge yourself when you look in the mirror? What are some ways you could be kinder to yourself?

Get Into Action

For the next thirty days, look in the mirror and say, "I love you."

Write it on your mirrors. Put Post-it notes up, saying things you like about yourself. Do your best not to say mean things about yourself. Pay attention to your speech. For example, instead of saying, "My _____ is fat or ugly", focus on something you do like and say, "My hair looks good today."

Our bodies hear everything we say.

Love your body. It will love you back.

Movie Recommendation: Watch the movie I Feel Pretty with Amy Poelher. It is one of the best examples I know to demonstrate how changing the way we feel about our bodies can radically transform our lives.

CHAPTER 3

Japan

LESSON:

Embrace Solitude

In 1993, I had just ended a five-year relationship with my boyfriend/business partner/best friend. Although we loved each other very much, we wanted different things from life. Looking back all these years later, I can definitely say it was one of the most important decisions I ever made.

I could have stayed. I could have settled into my comfortable life in a beautiful, affluent town in the Italian Alps. But these words still stay crystal-clear in my mind. My partner said to me, "If you stay here in this small town, you will resent me one day. The light will go out of your eyes. And I love you too much to let that happen."

So, he let me go. And off I flew, like a bird, first back to California, and then off to Asia, where I had applied for a job teaching English as a Second Language.

They say that the best way to move on after a break-up is to change your environment. Well, moving from Italy to Japan was a BIG cultural change.

I did not know any Japanese when I arrived in Tokyo. It was strange at first, living in a country where I did not speak the language. I immersed myself. I got by on sign language. I made a lot of Japanese friends who spoke a little English.

I had wonderful colleagues and students who treated me incredibly well. Teachers are highly respected in Japan, and I was no exception. I received gifts of gratitude from my students weekly. My company paid for my apartment, furniture, phone, transportation, and airfare. It was a convenient way to save money. Plus, I had a built-in social network, as Japanese companies highly encourage after-work activities such as karaoke, bowling, and eating and drinking together.

What changed me most in Japan was that it was the first time in all my life that I lived alone. The school I worked for gave me a studio apartment. Japan is a land of contrasts. Even though it is a small island populated with millions of people, many people live alone. It was the first place I ever went to a movie theater or out to a restaurant for lunch alone. There is no stigma in Japan around solitude.

Japanese people are often viewed as shy or quiet by foreigners. And yet, they are quite social once you get to know them. The Japanese language is full of pauses and silence. People wait to speak until you ask them a question. Introspection is something which is not only practiced, it is revered. Having an active imagination has been the impetus for Manga and so much of the Japanese fantasy games, art, and digital media.

In Japan, I learned the beauty of ZEN. (1) In a city as crowded and busy as Tokyo, going to the temple to sit in silence was a treat. It is there that I began the practice of meditation. Even though I did learn to speak Japanese, there were so many nuances I did not understand. Even with my close Japanese friends, there was much that went unsaid. It is a place where "reading between the lines" is practically an art form.

Being in Japan taught me so many wonderful things, but most importantly, I learned that being alone is not the same as being lonely – and silence is golden.

Reflection Questions

1. How do you feel about spending time alone? Is it something you love or fear? Why? Do you go places alone, like the movie theater or to a restaurant? How do you feel when you see someone sitting alone? Do you feel sorry for them?

2. Have you ever been to a place where you did not speak the language? How did you communicate? Were you afraid to make mistakes when you spoke? Why? Did you study another language in school? How often do you speak it or practice? Where could you go to practice?

3. If you had all of your expenses paid for one year, plus your salary, what would you do with all the money you saved?

4. What is your communication style? Do you listen more than you speak? Do you overlap or interrupt when others speak? Does this linguistic pattern run in your family? Do you get impatient with people who speak faster or slower than you do? What are some ways you could improve your communication with others?

Get Into Action

Choose one thing you will do alone each week. See how it feels. Keep doing it until the uncomfortable feeling goes away. Do not worry about being judged by others. If you have small children, find someone to babysit while you take some time alone to take care of yourself, such as getting a massage or reading a book. Self-care is vital to your health and well-being.

Movie Recommendation: For some comedy relief and to get an inkling of the Japanese art of reading between the lines, watch the movie Lost in Translation with Bill Murray.

CHAPTER 4
Cambodia

LESSON:
Compassion

The day was September 11, 2001.

I was sleeping at a guesthouse in Siem Reap, near Angkor Wat.

At 2:00 a.m., a Cambodian man knocked loudly on the door and yelled, "New York is on fire!"

I awoke startled and confused. Is this a dream or a nightmare?

My boyfriend and I shuffled into the main room, where there was a large cable TV. We watched, horrified, as the Twin Towers went up in smoke.

My mother and stepfather were living in Brooklyn at that time. So, my first thought was of them. Were they okay?

The Cambodians were kind to us and concerned. People who saw us later, walking through the streets, stopped to say, "I am sorry."

Cambodians understand tragedy. They have empathy for suffering. Pol Pot, a ruthless dictator, murdered over two million people in Cambodia during his reign in the 1970's. (1) Even decades later, the pain and suffering can still be felt there.

We were so sad and felt so helpless, being so far away from friends and family. There were no cell phones then, so the only way I could get a message through at two a.m. was to send an email.

The next day, we made our way to Phnom Penh, the capital of Cambodia.

While I am sure that things have improved since I was there, the situation in Phnom Penh was one of the worst I have ever encountered.

We were stopped countless times by strangers offering to sell us guns, children, and sex for hire with men, women, or children. We saw so many people who had lost an arm or leg to the many landmines left over from the Vietnam War.

I do not want to say that Cambodia is not a beautiful country. Angkor Wat is magnificent, full of ancient splendor and mysticism.

But my memories of that time are colored by sadness and grief.

What I remember vividly from that morning after the attack on New York City was our bus ride to Phnom Penh with a group of tourists from another country.

The girl sitting in front of us did not know we were American, and she said to her friend in a sarcastic fashion, "Those Americans, they deserve what happened to them."

I was livid. I wanted to punch her in the face. But I didn't. I don't remember exactly what I said, but I said something loudly in English to my boyfriend about how concerned I was about my family in New York and gave her the stink eye. She kept her opinions to herself for the rest of the trip.

I was shocked that someone could have so little compassion, especially coming from a neighboring country. If it could happen in New York City, it could happen in any city in North America or Europe.

The Cambodians showed us more kindness and compassion than our fellow Western travelers.

The lesson I learned here was COMPASSION. Like the adage says, "Love thy neighbor as thyself". I don't need to agree with my neighbors or even hang out with them. I don't need to vote the same party or invite them over for tea.

But I can still treat them with human decency and compassion.

We are all interconnected in our energy. So, when others feel pain, I feel pain. Compassion dissolves separation and brings us together. On September 11th, 2001 what was absolutely clear was how humanity came together to focus on support and love. Why must it take a tragedy for us to see that we are much more alike than we are different?

Reflection Questions

1. Where were you on 9/11/01? How did you feel on that day? How did that day change the way you viewed the world? Was anyone you know affected personally on that day? Did you feel more appreciation for your life? Your family? Your safety?

2. Think about your neighboring countries. What are you views of the people who live there? Do you have stereotypes and/or prejudices towards those people? How could you soften your views? Have you visited those countries? Did going to the country change your views for the better or for worse? Why?

3. Think about your neighbors where you live. Do you know their names? Are you friends with them? What do you know about their lives? Do you like them or not? Why? How could you get to know one or more of your neighbors better?

4. How much time do you spend watching the news on TV? How do you feel after watching it? Do you feel uplifted or depressed? What else could you do with your time besides watching the news?

Get Into Action

Choose a group of people you feel anger or fear towards.

Study more about their history, their circumstances, their challenges. If possible, visit their neighborhoods and/or countries. They say that ignorance breeds hate. So, learn as much as you can before making a judgment. What would it feel like to walk a day in their shoes? Look for ways they are similar to you. Try to soften your judgment and see what happens. See if your body feels different. Remember that anger, hate, and fear all affect our body in tangible and adverse ways.

CHAPTER 5

Thailand

LESSON:

Compassion

The year was 1996. I went to Thailand on a holiday after living in Japan for fifteen months. It was my first time traveling solo. However, I did not spend much of the trip alone. I met some Italians on the island of Koh Samui and traveled with them for several weeks.

After they departed home to Italy, I went up to Chiang Mai to go trekking through the jungle and visit the various hill tribes. On my trek were two Canadian girls, two New Zealanders, a German man, and one man, a stockbroker, from New York City. This is important for later in the story.

Some parts of the trek were brutal. It rained profusely, and we were soaked in mud much of the time.

The hill tribe people live in huts built of bamboo and palm. The conditions are very rustic. I recall one of my traveling mates getting a stomach virus and having to throw up in the outhouse on a mud floor with no plumbing. Oh, my heart went out to her.

The two things I enjoyed most about the trek were feeding and riding an elephant and the bamboo raft ride down the river. Our group had two rafts. The travelers on my raft were the "fun" members, and the other raft had the "serious" members. I was not very fond of listening to the stockbroker complain, and I thought some of my team members were far too serious and was glad they were on the other raft. Just to be mischievous, we decided to start a water fight with them to lighten the mood. By the end, everyone was laughing and having a great time. I find that laughter transforms even our darkest moods and brings out the inner child in all of us.

By the end of the trek, I was glad to get back to a hotel with warm water and a warm bed. Sleeping outdoors is adventurous but not something I like to do every day.

My flight home was in a few days, so I headed back to Bangkok. I had not been home in over a year and a half.

Upon arriving in Bangkok, I went to Khao San Road, where there are many cheap backpacker hostels, and left my bag at a hostel.

I was running low on cash, so I went to the ATM to get some money from my Visa card. I typed in the numbers and the machine read, "FUNDS DENIED". I tried several other banks and got the same message: "FUNDS DENIED." It was getting dark, and I was down to my last ten baht. That's about one U.S. dollar! I went into the bank, but the tellers did not speak English, and I only knew a few words in Thai. So, I started to panic.

I didn't know what to do. I had left my traveling companions back in Chiang Mai, and my other friends had already flown home. I called my parents collect several times, asking about the Visa card. They assured me that the card was fine, and there was money available.

It was almost dark. I had no money. So, I sat down on the street corner and cried.

Keep in mind that Bangkok is a HUGE, crowded city. It is not a place you want to be alone, female, and sleeping outside.

As I sat there, crying, I prayed and asked for help. I asked my angels to help me find a way to get through the night.

A few minutes later—I am not exaggerating—I heard someone call out to me in English. "Mica, is that you?" I looked up, and there on the crowded streets of Bangkok was the New York stockbroker, who had been in my trekking group. The one I was not particularly fond of. Ironically. God has a sense of humor.

He asked me why I was crying, and I explained what had happened at the bank. He said, "Here, take 100 baht for the night." I asked for his address to mail him the money, and he smiled. He said, "Hey, it's only ten bucks. No worries."

So, lesson number one: even people you don't particularly like can be a godsend.

I was so happy, I jumped up, hugged him, and thanked him

profusely. At least I would be able to pay for a hostel and not have to sleep outdoors.

I made my way back to the hostel. As I was checking in, the second group of angels found me. Down in the lobby, I ran into the two Canadian girls from the same trekking group. What a small world. They loaned me the cash for the airport tax, and later, I sent them a check when I got home.

My flight the next day was in the late afternoon, so in the morning, I took one last walk around the river. I passed by a bank and thought, Well, let's try this one more time...

This time, I went into the bank to ask the teller to withdraw the funds. I was in luck. This teller spoke a little English, so I asked for 100 baht. And she said, "Oh, miss, I am sorry, but that amount is too small. You can only withdraw in multiples of 500 baht or higher."

So, I said, "Okay, give me 500 baht." And bam—just like that, she ran the card and handed me the cash.

This lesson is a HUGE one, as it has served me many times in life.

ASK FOR MORE.

Sometimes, we are not getting what we want simply because we are expecting or asking for too little.

Angels are always here for us to help. When in doubt, ask for help. You will be surprised how many people will be willing to help you. And finally, don't stop just because you get a "NO". Keep trying. There is always a way around, under, or over a problem.

Reflection Questions

1. Think of a time you needed help, and it arrived in the form of a helpful stranger or friend. What did you learn from this experience?

2. Think of something you want but have not manifested yet. Are you asking for too little? Maybe the universe wants to give you more. What are some ways that you have not tried to get what you wish for?

3. Think of someone who made a poor first impression on you but then you warmed up to. Do you think that first impressions are always correct? Think of someone you don't like very much at school or at work and try to get to know them better. Decide if you have been correct in your original assessment or not.

4. Think of how much money you would like to earn/manifest this year? Take that number and double it. How do you feel when you look at that new number? Do you feel excited or afraid? Do some journaling on all of your limiting beliefs about money or people who have money.

Get Into Action

Step 1: Have you ever traveled solo? I challenge you to take one trip somewhere by yourself and make at least one new friend. Write about your experience in your journal.

Step 2: Find someone today that you don't know well whom you could help in a small way. Pay it forward. A small kindness can make a big difference in someone else's life.

CHAPTER 6

Fiji

LESSON:

Be Careful What You Wish For & Follow Your Intuition

It was June of 2002. Fiji was our last stop on a year-long backpacking trip. My boyfriend and I spent a total of five weeks on various islands. Fiji is absolutely gorgeous. One island we stayed on is where they filmed the original Blue Lagoon movie.

White sand, aqua-blue water, clear for miles, no people. Some of the remote islands required taking a small plane to get there.

The water was so clear and shallow that on our ride out to the islands, we saw a giant sea turtle swimming from the plane!

There are two really great stories from my trip to Fiji.

The first story involves me, a BIG shark, and a surprise.

While in Thailand a few months before, I had been practicing for my PADI Diving Certification but did not finish because I got sick and was hospitalized for hypothermia (another story for another day). I was very disappointed because one of my greatest wishes at that time was that I really, really wanted to swim with a shark. Well, "ask and ye shall receive". That wish came true several months later, when I was out swimming (alone) on a small Fijian island.

Early one morning, I decided to swim out to the coral reef before breakfast. So, I grabbed my fins and snorkel and dove in. I was happily floating around, watching the bright, colorful fish swim by, when I turned my head to see a sea snake—which are poisonous. I stopped several feet away and watched it swim by.

As it swam off to the left, I glanced beside me and saw a VERY large fish. At first, it did not register with me. And then my brain went, "THAT'S NOT A FISH—IT'S A SHARK!"

I was so stunned that at first, I didn't move. I just stared at it, trying to wrap my head around the fact that a reef shark bigger than me was looking right at me, and I was alone in the water. So, I did exactly what you are NOT supposed to do. I frantically started swimming to shore, gasping for breath, yelling, and swallowing water.

I made it to shore, shouting, "SHARK! SHARK!" The Fijian men came running with spears to catch it for dinner.

Alas, the shark had already swum away.

The Fijian men asked me what size it was. They said it was extremely rare that a reef shark would come so close to the shore, and they scratched their heads, wondering about it.

When I got to shore and told my boyfriend, he realized why the shark had come so close. Okay, graphic moment here, folks. I had my period. And sharks have such a keen smell for blood that the shark came to see what was for dinner. Now I am lucky because A., sharks do not attack unless they think they will win, which is why they leave dolphins alone. B., I was not injured. I was simply swimming with a tampon. C., There are a LOT of fish in Fiji for the shark to eat, so he was probably full.

Needless to say, if you make a wish for something, it will come. It may take days/weeks/years, but it will come.

They say, "Be careful what you ask for."

I say, "Be very, very specific." Now, when I ask for things, I am careful to add the words "Bring it to me GENTLY, please". I got my shark encounter, but it was way too close for comfort.

Second Lesson from FIJI:

Follow your intuition.

We were way out on remote islands, where there were no phones and no internet connection. Ah, the bliss of not knowing what is happening in the world. We had been in Fiji for several weeks.

One day, about a week before we were scheduled to leave, I woke up with a strong feeling in my body. It said, "Go back to the main island NOW!" I did not know why it was so strong or why I needed to go, but I always trust my gut. So, we took a boat back to Suva and checked our email for the first time in weeks.

And there it was. My mother had been desperately trying to contact me. My grandmother, whom I was very close to, had passed away. Her funeral was in Canada in a few days.

I called the airline, and they were able to get me on the flight going out the next day so that I would get there the morning of the funeral. This is quite a miracle because flights on Air New Zealand at the time were only going out from Suva once a week. So, if I had read my email even one day later, I would have missed the ceremony.

I arrived in time to give the eulogy for my dear Granny. There is absolutely no doubt in my mind that the message I got in Fiji was telepathic. It is not the first time I received messages telepathically, nor will it be the last.

I am so glad I was able to get back in time to speak at her ceremony about what a beautiful and beloved lady she was.

Fly with angels, Granny. I love you.

Reflection Questions

1. Think of something you really, really wanted to get or see that came true. What was it? How did you feel once you got it?

2. Did you ever ask for something but forget to be specific with the details and get more than you bargained for? What was it?

3. Have you ever gotten a strong feeling to do something without knowing why? Or received a message telepathically? Write the details in your journal. What happened when you listened to the message? What happened when you did not follow the message?

4. Have you ever had a close call with danger that you were somehow saved from? What did you learn from that experience? Why do you think you were saved? Do you believe in guardian angels?

CHAPTER 7

Germany

LESSON:

Listen to the Feedback

In the fall of 1992, I was finishing up my master's degree in International Economics in Milan. My boyfriend and I decided to start an import business in Italy. He was passionate about body-building and fitness, so we went to Germany for FIBO, the world's largest conference for fitness, wellness, and health. We wanted to see all the latest products, meet the vendors, and research the market. This was when the STEP in Aerobics had just become popular. Our idea was to import the STEP to Italy. We had already made a contract to become the distributors for CYBEX Fitness machines in Italy.

While at the conference, we found a product that my partner was extremely excited about. Let's call it the "VEST". It was a polyurethane vest with magnetic weights inside, so you could improve your endurance and stamina by working out with body weights.

However, I was thinking, *this product won't sell in Italy*. Gyms had just started popping up there, and people were still allowed to smoke at the gym. The women's workout apparel had shoulder pads in it. *No one will wear this vest. It is too bulky and too hot. Italians like to be fashionable, even at the gym.*

But my business partner and boyfriend was in love this this product. Why? Because he thought it would be a great product for him. As a basketball player who played on courts in California, it was indeed a great workout tool for him. But most people in Italy in the 1990's were not interested in becoming a sweaty mess. They wanted to look good at the gym. Wrong product, wrong time, wrong location.

This is a big life lesson for all of us. Just because you love something doesn't mean everyone else will too.

At the time, I strongly cautioned him. I said, "Test the market before launching. Order only a few demo vests, and take them to the gyms to see if there is any interest."

But he did not listen to me.

He ordered 100 vests. He spent $10,000 USD, which, adjusting for inflation, would equal $20,000 USD today.

Not one vest was ever sold.

Expensive lesson, no?

Those vests sat in a warehouse in Northern Italy for fifteen years, accumulating dust until they were donated to the local soccer league. Ironically, two decades later, the market was ripe with interest.

And speaking of timing, to make matters worse, in September of 1992, when we had just started our business, the Italian government devalued the Lire by 3.5-7%. (1) Therefore, our already expensive imported fitness products became even more pricey. Our only Italian competitor, which was selling at a much lower price, took over the market, and we were forced to close that business one year later.

Being an entrepreneur is a great teacher. Over the last twenty-five years, I have created and/or owned six different companies and a non-profit organization. For each of my businesses, I remembered this important lesson. I kept my overhead investment as low as possible and asked my clients what they wanted.

Moreover, when I taught business classes at the University of California San Diego, we spent several weeks each quarter learning about the importance of market research. Many a large and small company has lost thousands, sometimes millions, of dollars by not testing the market or listening to the feedback.

Do not assume that you can read other people's minds or that people will give you feedback without asking for it. Ask them what they want. Listen carefully. Give it to them if you are able. It is a simple rule which will save you a great deal of money, time, and energy.

Reflection Questions

1. When have you bought something you never used? Why did you buy it in the first place? Look in your closet right now and count how many items you have never used. Donate or sell them to someone who can/will use them as soon as possible.

2. Have you ever given good advice to someone close to you, and they ignored it? What happened? When is it appropriate to give advice to others? Do people ask for your advice?

3. Have you ever started or wanted to start your own company? Why kind of product or service would you offer? What need would it fulfill? Who is your target market? Who could you ask for advice to get your business plan ready? Have you looked into getting a business loan or grant from the government?

4. Have you ever received good advice and refused to listen? What happened? What did you learn? Are you good at receiving feedback? Do you shut down or get angry at the messenger? Is this serving your highest good?

Action Step

Ask for feedback.

In leadership training, I learned that feedback makes me stronger, not weaker. No one likes to get negative feedback, but not changing a negative habit does not make it miraculously disappear.

Here are some questions to ask at least five people that you know.

Be sure to ask at least one work colleague, one supervisor, and one mentor or teacher. Your friends or family might not tell you the whole truth for fear of upsetting you. The first time might be uncomfortable, but over time, you will see that the benefits are worth it.

1. What do you think is my best quality? Why?
2. What do you think is my biggest weakness? Why?
3. Where do you see me holding myself back?
4. To improve our relationship/communication, what is one thing I could do differently?

Listen with big ears. Ask regularly. You will be amazed at how much your relationships will improve by practicing this technique.

CHAPTER 8

Switzerland

LESSON:

Hospitality

From 2005 to 2015, I taught business and writing to the international students at UC San Diego. During that time, I mentored thousands of students from thirty-three different countries. One student I met from Switzerland was Carmen Balmer. When she left San Diego, she gave me a coupon for a free night's stay at her hostel in Interlaken. I kept the card since I went to Switzerland often to visit friends.

In 2015, I was in Lugano, visiting friends, and I decided to take a day trip over to Interlaken. So, I sent Carmen a message on Facebook. I love that it is so easy now to connect with friends all over the world this way.

She replied excitedly to come and visit and be her guest.

When I arrived at the little train station, deep in the middle of the Alps, I was met by Carmen and her dad. They immediately took me to have some champagne. After all, why not start an adventure with a champagne toast? Erich Balmer, her father, was driving a renovated bus from World War II to show me around the town.

They took me to various spots: the hostel, the skydiving camp, the restaurant, the bungee jumping park, all of which, to my surprise, they own and operate. What I didn't know is that Erich Balmer is to travel in Switzerland like Oreo is to cookie.

So, the first lesson I want to highlight here is: you never know who you will meet on your journeys. Stay open.

Erich and Carmen were lovely hosts, and I hope that you will visit their hostel, Balmer's, in the beautiful town of Interlaken (www.balmers.com). I am very grateful for the hospitality they showed me. In fact, all over the world, so many people have invited me into their homes.

Second lesson: if someone invites you to their country, say "YES".

Of course, you need to trust your gut if it feels uncomfortable to you. But of all the countries I have visited and all the friends I have stayed with, I have never had a bad experience. Not once.

Staying in people's homes is different from staying in a hotel. You get to eat local food and see how they view the world.

It's a beautiful thing.

Every time I have been to Switzerland, I have been hosted and treated with the utmost hospitality. I want to give a special shout-out of gratitude to Carmen, Angela, Aicha, and Natasha, who have hosted me at their homes in Switzerland. Thank you for your warm hearts and warm hospitality.

Like the Beatles sang, we get by with a little help from our friends.

Reflection Questions

1. Have you ever hosted anyone from another country in your home? Are you open to it? Why or why not?

2. Have you stayed in someone else's home abroad? How did you feel? What did you learn? How was their home the same or different from your home?

3. Where have you been invited that you could say "YES" to? Have you ever said no to an invitation, then regretted it afterwards? Why? Have you ever said YES and then regretted it afterwards? Why?

Get Into Action

SAY YES to every invitation you get for the next thirty days.

SIDE-NOTE

In 2015, I had a coach who challenged me to do this. I went on the first date with my future husband while I was taking this challenge. I might have said NO because he did not seem like my usual "type". But I said yes. What opportunities lie ahead for you? Just be open to the possibility. Get out of your comfort zone. Follow your gut, be aware. Don't accept offers that feel dangerous. But give the "maybes" a chance.

CHAPTER 9

Spain

LESSON:

Tell the Truth Faster

In 1988, I moved to Madrid, Spain as an exchange student to study at the Complutense University. I lived there for over a year. There are many wonderful places to visit in Spain. It is, by far, one of the liveliest and most enjoyable places I have ever been--full of history, art, architecture, delicious food, and an incredible night-life. I do not know how I got anything done at school because I do not recall sleeping much at all.

But the story I want to share for this chapter is about love—or, more specifically, unrequited love.

While I lived in Madrid, I made several close and dear friends, one of whom was a kind man named Pablo.*

When I first met him, I could tell that he was attracted to me, so I quickly informed him that I had a boyfriend in California who was coming to visit me soon.

He said, "No problem. I would like to get to know him too." So, when my boyfriend came to Spain to visit, I introduced them to each other. They became fast friends and are still friends all these years later.

Have you ever had a crush on someone who was "unavailable"? If you are like most people, then the answer is probably "yes".

So, Pablo and I became friends, and he and my boyfriend and I often went out together. Later, when I left Spain, he stayed in touch and wrote to me often.

Now, I always knew that he had feelings for me all those years. But I did not feel the same way.

But the story did not end there. Fast-forward to the winter of 2003. I was living in Seoul, Korea (which will be covered in another chapter). It was cold and snowy. I was sad, recovering from a broken heart, and lonely. And my friend from Spain still wrote to me often to see how I was doing.

For those of you who are female and single, have you felt a strong pull to get married and have children by a certain age? I felt it, BIG TIME!

At this point, I was thirty-four, and here was this kind man who wanted to take care of me, marry me, make babies with me, and treat me like a queen. It all sounded so very tempting at the time.

He invited me to come back to Spain to visit him. Mind you, I had not been there since 1989, fourteen years prior. And this man had kept the torch burning all those years.

I was thinking, well, what do I have to lose? I might feel differently all these years later. But to him, it was different. He was imagining that his dream would come true, that dream he had held since we met years before.

Did you ever hold a fantasy in your mind about someone that was greater than the reality?

Now you are probably guessing what happened.

I did go back to Spain and visit him. He was a perfect gentleman. He was kind and generous and gallant, just as he had always been.

But alas, I did not have those same feelings. I could not feel an attraction which wasn't there. I wished at the time that I did, just so I would not have to hurt him.

I could never live up to that pedestal which he put me on. I could never create feelings as intense as his, which had been burning for years.

Chemistry is a funny thing. They say, scientifically, that if you don't feel it in the beginning, you won't feel it later. One needs a spark to make a fire.

So, I told him I could not stay, and he was very upset. He did not forgive me for many years. I hope that he is happy now and has met a good woman who can give him the love he so deserves. I chose to end things before they started. Why? It hurt him when I told him the truth, but it would have hurt him far worse if I had pretended.

He wanted forever. I just couldn't give it to him.

They say Karma is a b***h. All that we do comes back to us sooner or later, including the pain we inflict. I was on the receiving end of this scenario later on in my life. Living on the other side of this equation gave me even more compassion for him. But it also showed me why ending it early had been the best decision in the long run.

I learned such a very important lesson about love. Love needs to be equal, not just convenient. Commitment is an everyday exercise, and there needs to be a lot of glue to hold it together. If there is no chemistry, sooner or later, someone will stray. Hearts will get broken.

Tell the truth sooner, even if it is painful. Tell yourself the truth. And tell the other person the truth. They deserve that much from you.

A clean break heals much faster than a jagged, deep wound.

Reflection Questions

1. Have you ever felt pressure to settle into a relationship with someone you did not love?

2. Have you ever loved someone who did not love you back equally?

3. Have you ever hidden or hesitated telling the truth to someone because you knew it would hurt them? Was it better to wait longer? What were the consequences?

4. Karmically, think of something you did to someone that came back to you? How did it feel to be on the receiving end?

5. Can you forgive those exes who have hurt you? How much value is there in holding on to a grudge or broken heart?

Get Into Action

Write or call someone you have hurt, directly or indirectly.
Apologize from the heart. They will be able to feel if you are
sincere or not. Make amends. If that person is no longer alive
or you do not know how to contact them, write a letter anyway.
Energy is interesting. When there is an open wound, it leaves
a loose end inside of us. By asking for forgiveness, we may or
may not receive it, but it will actually heal us. Energy cords
connect us to others. Making amends seals the energy leaks.
Forgive yourself. And move on.

Book Recommendation: *Calling in the One* by Katherine
Woodward Thomas is by far one of the best books I have ever
read on healing our past wounds and choosing relationships
from a place of wholeness.

CHAPTER 10

Bahamas

LESSON:

How to Mend a Broken Heart

It was December 2011. I arrived in the Bahamas with a broken heart.

At the end of 2010, I broke up with a man I had been dating for about a year and a half. I was forty-three at the time, and I thought my time was running out to have a baby. I asked him point-blank if he was ready, and he said, "No."

So, it was time to move on. After much thought and research, I decided to pursue having a baby on my own. Yes, I live in a place where this is legal, available, and growing in popularity.

I truly wanted to have a baby with a loving partner. I just kept choosing people who were not ready. I used the word "choosing" because for so many years, I have heard myself and other women say that men are afraid of commitment. The cold, hard truth is that men are not commitment-phobic. Look around the world. Men are getting married and making babies at all ages from teens to even in their seventies. Men are not the issue.

I was the commitment-phobe. Therefore, I was attracting men just like me.

At this point in my life, however, I really thought I was ready to make a commitment to motherhood.

Physically and consciously, I was ready. But subconsciously, as you will see, I was not.

I went to the sperm bank in San Diego (a sentence I never imagined I would say or write). Oh, how modern things have become. I chose the best donor based on his physical and personality characteristics. This donor had an excellent track record, and there are quite a few babies in San Diego who have been fathered by him.

I did acupuncture weekly and followed a detox diet for one year. I visualized and followed all the natural fertility protocols. My doctors were amazed at my egg count. They asked me often if I took drugs to boost my fertility, to which I replied confidently—and almost smugly—that I do not need to take drugs. At forty-four, my ovaries were full of egg follicles growing!

I did everything right. Everything. I went through all the procedures, ultrasounds, tests, etc. every month for six months.

My ovulation was right on schedule at fourteen days exactly, my uterine lining was excellent, all the perfect conditions, but NO baby.

By the end of 2011, I had spent all my savings and was severely exhausted and frustrated. There was nothing physically wrong with my body, but something psychologically was blocking me. I felt stuck.

I did the only thing I could do. I let go, surrendered and gave myself a much-needed break.

In December, right before Christmas, I flew to the Bahamas.

Once there, all I did every day was go to the ocean, go to the jacuzzi, and take a bath. Like a fish, I spent almost all my time in the water.

Why does water heal us? Many studies show how soaking, drinking, and immersing ourselves in water and being near the ocean is healing. (1)(2) Dr. Masaru Emoto's famous study of water demonstrates just how alive water actually is. (3) Immersing yourself in water literally makes you feel better. And having a good, long cry is our body's way of purging negative energy.

After seven days and eight nights of soaks, I was feeling more like myself again. I am an eternal optimist, and hope floats.

I realized that I still had time, and I really did not want to be a single mom. My hat's off to the single moms reading this book. Parenting is a difficult job, and doing it alone is even harder.

I was grateful that my body was strong and fertile, but I was pushing too hard, trying to control the outcome. In my heart of hearts, I really wanted a partner who loved me and who wanted to create a family together. I had to surrender control to the manager upstairs. Let go. Let God.

I am so thankful for the beautiful blue water of the Bahama Islands, to the kind people I met, and especially to the man who sat down next to me on the beach and shared his story with me. He was a recovering heroin addict, now a yoga teacher. After hearing his story and what he went through in rehab, it made me see that even though life had not gone the way I wanted, things could be so much worse!

And as it drew closer to Christmas, on Dec 23rd, I thought to myself, *what am I doing here, on a beach by myself, when I have a family who wants to celebrate Christmas with me?* So, I left early and arrived in time to surprise my parents on Christmas Eve.

The next time life brings you down, and things don't go the way you want, remember life could be worse. And there is another day to try, try again. As you will read in a later chapter, I did eventually get my wish to meet the man who wanted to create a family with me. Don't ever lose hope.

Reflection Questions

1. Think of a time you wanted something to happen on your time schedule. Looking back at that moment, did the universe have a better plan for you?

2. Do you feel you are running out of time? Is your biological clock ticking? Is it really true that you are running out of time? With all the new technologies in medicine, are you willing to freeze your eggs? How do you feel about assisted reproductive technology? Do you know anyone who has tried it? Do they have children now? What are the advantages of being able to do a DNA test before pregnancy (in other words, screening the eggs and sperm for specific abnormalities or a predisposition to specific diseases)?

3. What are the advantages and disadvantages of being a single parent? Do you think it is always best to stay together in a marriage, even if the relationship is dysfunctional or abusive, just for the sake of the children? What was your experience growing up? Did both of your parents live with you at home? Did they get along? How did their choices affect you?

4. What are some of the advantages and disadvantages of being an older mother? A younger mother? For those of you who are in your twenties and had your children young, what is something you wish you had known or done differently?

Get Into Action

Step 1: If there is something you really want but have been holding back because you are afraid of what other people might think, consider taking a leap and doing it anyway. If you never try, you will never know.

Step 2: Go swim or put your feet in the ocean. If you do not live near the water, buy some sea salt or Epsom salt and have a bath. Immerse yourself in it and soak for a while. Let the salt bath cleanse your worries away. Look up Edgar Cayce's holistic cures using Epsom salts and castor oil packs. (4) I have used them often and have found them to be very effective.

CHAPTER 11

Croatia

LESSON:

Be Prepared When Opportunity Knocks

In 1989, I was living in Madrid, Spain, studying at the Complutense University on a year-long exchange program with the University of California (UC).

Near the end of the school year, there was a contest for one student to represent the international students in the UC Education Abroad Program Annual Conference in Dubrovnik, Croatia. In order to be chosen, there was an interview with the director of the head of the EAP program in Madrid.

At this point in my life, I was a college senior majoring in

Political Science and International Relations. I spoke Spanish more fluently than most of the other UC students whom I was competing against. I thought I had it in the bag. I was so sure that I would win the competition that I did not even bother to prepare—which was a BIG mistake.

I walked into the interview, and the first question the director asked me was about something which had happened that morning in Madrid. I expected to be asked about the Euro or something pertaining to European Politics. Needless to say, I did not know the answer, nor did I get chosen as the representative.

The lesson I learned poignantly was to be prepared next time opportunity knocked—and to be humbler when given another chance.

I did get another chance.

Upon returning to UC Santa Barbara and graduating with my B.A., I received a call from my former boss, who was president of the local Santa Barbara Rotary Club. He asked me if I were interested in applying for a scholarship to be an Ambassador of Goodwill to represent the United States abroad for the Rotary International Foundation.

I was absolutely interested! And I vowed to myself to be TRIPLE-prepared. I stayed up late into the night writing my application essay and had it proofread and edited several times. Plus, I practiced for the in-person interview with a Rotarian who had been on the choosing committee in years past.

This time, I went into the interview calm, humble, and hopeful.

Being prepared paid off, as I was chosen to go to Italy for one year on a full scholarship. The scholarship paid for my Italian language studies in Florence and Rome, as well as the Master's Degree Program at the renowned Luigi Bocconi School of Business in Milan, Italy. It was the opportunity of a lifetime, and I grabbed it with gusto.

So, you see, I missed my chance for a weekend in Dubrovnik, but that lesson served me well. I was given a much bigger opportunity later. One door closes, and another one opens.

Be humble, be open, and be on the lookout! Wonderful opportunities are just waiting for you to say YES.

Reflection Questions

1. When have you missed out on something you really wanted?
   Why did you miss the chance?

2. How could you have been better prepared? What do you think
   stopped you from being successful?

3. How will you prepare/act differently when opportunity
   knocks again?

4. Have your ever applied or received a scholarship or grant to
   further your studies? If you were given the chance, where
   would you go? What would you study? Why?

Get Into Action

Google "Scholarships/Grants for Graduate or University Study". Look up all the scholarships/grants available and read the requirements. For each one that you qualify for, send in an application. Not all scholarships are based on financial status. Some are based on gender, area of study, talent, or academic skill. Every year, tens of thousands of dollars in scholarships go unused because people simply do not apply.

CHAPTER 12

Costa Rica

LESSON:

Emotions Affect Our Health

*"You cannot heal
what you cannot feel."*
-Louise Hay

I visited Costa Rica twice—first in 1997, and the second time in 2007. Both times, I learned life-changing lessons.

Let's talk first about the visit in 2007.

I flew down to Costa Rica for my friend Gaby's wedding. At

the time, I had a part-time business in photography, so my gift to the bride was to take her wedding photos. It is important to note that for most of my younger years, being at weddings gave me an upset stomach. Growing up with divorced parents, the idea of marriage still made me uneasy. I chose to become a wedding photographer on purpose. I was determined to change how I felt about the concept of marriage. As I flew down to Costa Rica, I visualized how much fun I was going to have at this wedding.

I flew into the capital, San José, and made my way to the bus station to catch a local bus to Tamarindo. As I waited, I opened a book I had been wanting to read for quite some time. It was called *Three Cups of Tea*. The story is about a man, Greg Mortenson, who gets injured while climbing in the Himalayas and is cared for by a Pakistani tribe. He stays for weeks to recover and falls in love with the people there—so much so that he vows to help build a school for the girls in this small village, who have not had access to an education. He ends up building many schools in both Pakistan and Afghanistan. I was so moved and inspired by his story—it planted a seed in my mind. Two years later, I would go to Africa, as you have already read, and start building schools for children as well.

Stories are like that, planting seeds in your mind to take root later, hopefully in the most marvelous ways.

Back in Costa Rica, I made my way to Tamarindo and had a splendid time. It was the first wedding that I thoroughly enjoyed. Seeing the couple and their friends and family dancing and having so much fun at the beach, under the stars, transformed my image of what a wedding could be like. Another seed planted.

Now let's go back to the first time I went to Costa Rica, in 1997.

You will see how, in a weird and brilliant way, everything in life is connected.

I went to Costa Rica with a man I was dating; let's call him Robert*. He is and was very talented, handsome, romantic, adventurous, and successful—everything I thought I wanted. Except for one thing: when we traveled together, we fought like cats and dogs.

We were staying in this incredible house in the middle of the Manuel Antonio rain forest, where monkeys come eat breakfast with you on your patio. It was so beautiful and lush. Unfortunately, however, I cried most of the trip. At one point, I had a urinary tract infection that was so painful, I was peeing blood. (Louise Hay, in her life-changing book *You Can Heal Your Life*, says that UTIs are caused when we are "pissed off" at our partners. Boy, was she right.) (1)

Robert and I dated on and off for three and a half years. We weren't happy together, but we just couldn't seem to let go. Unfortunately, sometimes we humans need a kick in the butt to do what needs to be done. My big wake-up call came in 1998 when my doctor discovered cancer cells on my cervix, the opening of the uterus. Another disease in the same area of my body (2nd Chakra). My body was sending me a signal, and the signal was getting LOUDER. I knew that I had to change something. And I had to do it decisively. The cancer was at Stage 3, which is very serious. Thank God I was getting annual check-ups every year. If we had not caught it early, I might not have lived to write this story.

There are several important and possibly life-saving lessons here. I hope you learn them without having to get sick.

First, if your relationship is making you miserable or sick all the time, end it. The person might be great, but if you are feeling terrible inside of your relationship, get out or get counseling. Your life and your health are way more important than anything else. Even if you have children, they need you to be healthy and alive, so don't stay in a relationship that is hurting you physically or emotionally.

Second, and I repeat this just in case you didn't get it the first time: if your body sends you a wake-up call, pay attention. There are no accidents. Your body is always talking to you. I manifested several diseases in the same place over and over until I finally made the mind-body-emotion connection.

I am happy to report that since 1998, all of my pap scans have been clear.

Finally, to connect all the dots here, fast-forward twenty years. Robert and I are still friends. In fact, we are much better as friends than we ever were as romantic partners. The universe, in its infinite wisdom, always brings us exactly who we need to learn from to get to the next chapter in our lives.

Over the years, we have collaborated on several projects. Most notably, together, we have helped build several schools for orphaned children. He helped me raise thousands of dollars to build and support the Good Hope School in Uganda, Africa. And recently, he built two schools in Asia.

Can you see how it all gets back to those THREE CUPS OF TEA?

Books are powerful. Seeds are being planted right now, in you, while you are reading this book.

Reflection Questions

1. Which books have you read that changed your life? How did they change you? Be specific.

2. Have you ever dated or lived with someone who wasn't good for you, but you had a hard time letting go? What did you learn from that person?

3. Do you have any toxic relationships in your life now? With family, friends or romantic partners? Are you willing to leave these relationships for the sake of your health? Why or why not? If not, are you willing to seek counseling to help you move forward?

4. Think back to some illnesses you have had in the past. Were you angry at the time? Or sad? Who were you angry at or disappointed in? Do you see a connection between your health and your emotions? Do you frequently get sick in one particular part of your body, such as your throat or stomach? What emotion might you be repressing or holding onto in that part of your body?

Get Into Action

Step 1: Make a list of all the illnesses you have had in the last ten to twenty years. Take special note of recurring illnesses and which section of the body they occurred in. Look up the Seven Chakra System on the internet. (2) Each chakra is associated with a different emotion and/or purpose. For example, the throat is related to expressing your voice/telling the truth and the stomach is related to personal power. Do some research on this topic to discern what is out of balance in your system. Emotions that are not expressed go inward and cause imbalance and disease. Get to the root emotional cause before your body gives you a LOUD wake-up call.

Step 2: Make an appointment with your doctor to get an annual check-up. Many sexually transmitted diseases and types of cancer do not have any overt symptoms, so take the tests. It's better to be safe than sorry.

Book Recommendation: *You Can Heal Your Life*
 by Louise Hay
Movie Recommendation: Heal (Documentary)

CHAPTER 13

Canada

LESSON:

Connection

The year was 1967, and I was born three months early in a hospital in Vancouver. My identical twin sister weighed almost two pounds, and I weighed three pounds. That's super premature! Many babies at that weight do not survive, especially not in the 1960s.

They put me in an incubator for three months. Back then, parents were not allowed into the NICU (Neo-Natal Intensive Care Unit). Only the nurses could hold or touch us. My sister was separated from me because her organs were failing. She only lived for a few days, but one never loses connection with one's twin, especially not identical twins who share the same DNA.

I cannot imagine what it was like for my parents standing outside the glass of the NICU, fearful and helpless to save us. Only a miracle could do that. The technology nowadays is much more advanced. They might have been able to save her today. But she went to heaven and has been my guardian angel ever since. There have been so many studies done on twins and how closely they are connected emotionally and telepathically. (1)(2) I have always felt her presence. Like a phantom limb, I felt her even though her physical body was gone.

So, the first lesson I learned at a very early age is: people can feel each other empathically and telepathically. Having grown with my twin in the womb, I never felt disconnected or afraid of people. Connecting with others empathically always felt natural to me. While doing research for my master's degree in Education, I spent many years studying the brain to better understand how telepathy and empathy work. I believe that in the future we will learn more ways to communicate telepathically, and possibly use even telepathy more than verbal communication.

Above all, I feel deeply blessed to have had my twin sister as my guide and guardian angel all these years. Thank you, dear sister, for all the times you sent me inspiration and messages.

We left Canada when I was one year old to move to California. However, I went back every year to visit and stay with my grandparents in the beautiful city of Victoria.

I have so many happy memories of summers there with them. I was their only grandchild, and we had so many adventures together. Many people I knew growing up were not close to their grandparents. They lived far away and saw each other infrequently. I think this is a loss for the children of the world who do not know their grandparents. I spent amazing days exploring lakes, gorges, parks, gardens, and glaciers with my grandparents. They also had a glorious fruit garden, so my grandmother taught me to make jams, jellies, and pies. Those were some of the happiest memories of my childhood, summers in Canada, outside in nature.

This leads to the second great lesson I learned as a child: spending time in nature is imperative. Being out in the fresh air with the trees makes us healthier. It calms us and grounds us. (3) With the increase of dependence on technology, many children spend more time inside, interacting with a box. And yet, people are surprised that there is less respect for the environment and child obesity levels are on the rise.

Moreover, being out in nature teaches us the connection between what we grow and what we eat. Children learn their eating habits from their parents. We have a responsibility to show them how to thrive.

In most cities, food is packaged, processed, fried, and/or full of chemical additives. How can one teach a child about healthy eating if one does not know what healthy eating looks like? Nowadays, I have a large organic garden and eat mostly fruit and vegetables. Eating organic is a choice. It is one of my anti-aging secrets. I am connected to what I put into my body. When you grow your own food, you become much more connected to what is going into your body. Plus, the food tastes much better.

Grow a garden. Nurture a plant. Go outside and lie on the grass.

Reflection Questions

1. Who do you feel a strong connection with? Do you know what they are thinking sometimes? Do you feel their suffering? Do you believe it possible to communicate telepathically? Why or why not?

2. What is your connection/relationship with your siblings/ grandparents? Are you close or estranged? What do you wish you could say to them? What important lessons did you learn from your grandparents/siblings while growing up?

3. When was the last time you went outside and sat under a large tree? Or picnicked in a park? Or hiked in a canyon? If you live in the city, where could you go to get in touch with some nature? Go there today.

4. How green is your diet? How could you incorporate more vegetables or fresh foods into your meals? If you have children, what kinds of eating habits are you showing them? How is your diet affecting your health? Positively or negatively? What are some ways you could eat healthier?

Get Into Action

Activity 1: Start growing a plant or garden. Speak words of encouragement and thanks to your plants. Watch how they grow. Imagine that the plant is your body. Treat it well, and give it water and sunlight. As you nurture the plant, you nurture yourself.

Activity 2: If one of your loved ones has transitioned, I encourage you to write them a letter telling them all the things you want to share. You could put the message in a bottle and release it to the sea or burn or bury it. If you are feeling strong emotions such as rage or resentment, this process will help you transmute your painful emotions and let go.

Movie Recommendation: Forks Over Knives (Documentary)

CHAPTER 14

Malaysia

LESSON:

Boundaries

In 2002, while crossing the border between Thailand and Malaysia by bus, I looked out the window and saw a HUGE sign with a warning on it. It is big and brutal and obvious. It said, "DRUG USERS will be HUNG".

It showed a man with a noose around his neck.

Wow! that image is forever etched in my memory.

It was a direct message for all the backpackers crossing the border. Thailand is a place where people go to have fun and enjoy all-night parties. There is a lot of drinking and recreational drug use. Thailand has laws against this, but they are not strictly enforced.

Malaysia, however, a Muslim country, has a NO tolerance policy for drugs.

As brutal as it was to see a sign with a man hanging from a noose. I have to say it was effective. It sent a loud and visceral message to tourists. "This is our boundary, and it must be respected!"

I had a lovely time in Malaysia, especially on the island of Tioman and in Georgetown, wandering around Chinatown. The Cameron Highlands, with its vast green tea fields, are a nice respite from the city and humidity.

When in Rome (or Malaysia), do as the Romans do. Over the years traveling, I have learned to respect the culture of the country I am in. It is, after all, I who am a visitor in their country and not the other way around. There is a stereotype of the "ugly American" who travels abroad, demanding and expecting life to be just like at home. I travel to learn, not to experience the status quo. If I want things to be and look the same, I stay at home.

Malaysia teaches a clear lesson about boundaries. If you want to do drugs, go somewhere else. I teach people how to treat me. If I hold a clear expectation of how I want to be treated, people will feel that. They will either respect that boundary or gravitate away from me. People with a poor sense of boundaries usually have many complaints about how people don't listen to them, how someone took advantage of them, how someone broke their promises, etc. But, look closely at the boundaries they set. Loose boundaries create chaotic energy. No exceptions.

As an elementary and high school teacher, I learned this lesson well. Kids are good at wearing people down to get what they want. They will yell, scream, cry, hurl insults, and throw tantrums to demand what they want. Parents, are you feeling me here?

How strong is your "NO"? Malaysia does not waver. I respect that. How strong are the boundaries you are setting with your children, your colleagues, your friends and family members? Children have an uncanny knack for sniffing out where the boundary is weak, so look to them to give you a mirror of where your boundaries could be clearer.

People will treat you with the same energy you treat yourself.

Reflection Questions

1. How clear are your boundaries? Is your "NO" a real "no"? Or do you waffle? Do you cave in when pestered? Why? Is it because of guilt? How could you practice giving firmer YESes and firmer NOs?

2. Do you find that people respect your boundaries or often disregard them? Do you respect other people's boundaries? Think of a person in your life who exemplifies clear boundaries. Is that person having more success in their life? How could you emulate them?

3. As a parent, do you give clear directions or change your mind? Are you a good example of what healthy boundaries look like? How is your lack of clear boundaries affecting your home life? For example, when it comes to going to bed or doing homework, it is a constant struggle? Look at ways you could incorporate more structure into these routines so that they can be more enjoyable.

Get Into Action

Choose one area where your boundaries are too lax. You will know which one because it will be an area of constant frustration for you. It could be a boundary with yourself, like keeping a promise you've made, or a boundary with someone else, such as bedtime for your kids.

Example: I have a "no cell phones during meals" policy with everyone, especially my thirteen-year-old stepson. To maintain this, I turn my own phone off and put it away. I give people my full attention which shows respect for them and also creates an atmosphere of trust. How do you feel when you are at dinner and the other person is looking at their cell phone more than at you?

CHAPTER 15

Tahiti

LESSON:

Destiny

This is a story I recounted in my father's eulogy in 2015. This book would not be complete without one of his marvelous travel anecdotes. I would not be who I am today without having learned so much from him.

So, let me go back in time a bit. My father studied at the Italian Naval Academy in Venice in the 1950's. He then joined the Italian Merchant Marine and sailed all over the world. He often said, "If there is a port in that country, I've been there." While growing up, he often regaled me with fantastic stories of his travels.

One of my favorite stories was of his visit to the island of

Tahiti. Imagine an island so beautiful, it looks like heaven. Then picture it even more beautiful, and that is Tahiti. Paul Gauguin, one of my favorite painters, lived there for years, capturing the bright colors and exotic beauty.

In the fifties, there were very few tourists there. The island was inhabited by the local Tahitian tribes. Like Hawaii, Tahiti has a royal family and a chief. My father, with his naval uniform and his Italian good looks, must have looked so handsome to the local Tahitian women. He and his fellow sailor and friend, Francesco, went onshore and stayed in Tahiti for more than three months.

The way my father told the story was like this…

Francesco had met one of the king's daughters, who was quite smitten. So, Francesco invited my dad to the royal complex to meet the king. I do not know how long they stayed at the palace, but I do know that the king liked my father so much that he asked him to stay in Tahiti and marry one of his daughters, a princess.

Wow! That's what I call a travel adventure. I am sure my father was very flattered. But he declined. He was too much of an adventurer to settle down at that point. He was young, handsome, carefree, and sailing around the world. Would you say "no" to a king? He did.

All I can say is that I am glad he refused because if he had said "yes", I would never have been born. He would have stayed in Tahiti and never been on a cargo ship from Russia to Canada, which stopped over in Victoria, where he met my mother.

My father was an adventurer and visionary who left his small town in Southern Italy to see the world. It is his DNA that was passed on to me. In the photo section of this book, you will see him in front of the Buddha at Kamakura. Years later, when I lived in Japan, I went to that very same place.

I had to include one of his stories to show you why I became the person I am. We all carry pieces of our parents inside of us. He has now left this world and is no doubt sailing around on adventures in heaven. I thank him from the bottom of my heart for having given me his "travel" gene and for working to create a better life for me. I carry him in my heart always.

Tahiti is high on my wish list. Maybe I will tell you the story of my adventures there in my next book.

Reflection Questions

1. How and when did your parents meet? Do you know their story? Ask them to tell you, if possible.

2. In what ways are you like your mother or your father? Write them down. Ask yourself if these qualities are benefitting you or burdening you.

3. Think of a significant moment in your life when you had to make a big choice. How would your life be different if you had chosen the other path? Who would be affected and how?

....

....

....

4. What is something that your mother or father did that you, too, would like to do? Plan to do it within the next year. Last year, I learned to sail just like my papa. It's never too late to learn something new.

....

....

....

Get Into Action

Write out a family tree. Contact family members and find out at least one significant story from their life to remember and pass on. If possible, interview them on video. Since my father's passing, I often listen to the recordings we made. Just hearing his voice makes me smile and cry—but mostly smile.

CHAPTER 16

Turkey

LESSON:

Read the Signs

On New Year's Day 2015, I flew into Istanbul very early in the morning. A new year, a new city, and a new start. I was greeted at the airport by one of my favorite former students, Duygu, whom I am blessed to call a friend.

The first place she took me to was a delightful restaurant with incredible food overlooking the famous Bosphorus Straight called "HAPPILY EVER AFTER". It was a sign!

I exhaled, hugged my friend, and knew that somehow everything was going to be okay.

The end of 2014 had been fraught with stress. My father had

been diagnosed with a rare form of lung cancer, and the man whom I had been sort of dating long-distance got cold feet when things got serious. I had known him for many years as a friend, so I wasn't exactly surprised. People always show you who they are if you pay attention.

Fortunately, by this point in my life, I had become much more adept at heeding the signs sooner rather than later. I did not waste much energy or time trying to fix a confirmed bachelor. I simply hopped on a plane from Rome to Istanbul and did not look back. Good, bad, gentle, harsh, the Universal GPS is always sending us signs to indicate if we are ON or OFF course.

In Istanbul, I stayed at the home of my Turkish soul sister, Sevecen. When we met in San Diego, back in 2006, we immediately had a soul connection. We even look like sisters. One day, when she invited me over to her home for the first time, we discovered that we had a mutual talent for reading the oracles. Sevecen reads the coffee cup oracle, and I read the oracle cards. We often used to do readings for each other and laugh and cry. Even if we don't speak the same native language, we always understand each other.

She often told me about a "famous" oracle reader in Istanbul. I really wanted to visit her. So, in 2015, I had my chance.

This Turkish healer did not speak English, and I did not speak Turkish, so Sevecen was our translator. We spent a total of three hours in our session with her. She used a combination of oracles and healing crystals, and I wrote down everything Sevecen translated.

That lady, in a little apartment on the eastern side of Istanbul, gave me page after page of information. Everything she said was spot-on! The predictions she made have already come to pass. She saw my wedding and my future husband. She saw the books I would write and the places I would visit. It was POWERFUL.

Many of you reading this book might not believe in oracles or psychics. That's fine. I am not here to convince you. What I do want to implant in your brain is that if you ask a question, the answer will come. Sometimes, it comes in a book you read or a song you hear. It might even come via a stranger's words or from a teacher you trust. It does not matter if you believe in oracles. Believe that if you need an answer, it will come to you in a way that you understand.

Ask and pay attention.

I asked that woman many questions that day, and I continue to ask the universe questions every day, even mundane questions like which food is best for my body or which insurance policy is best for my car or which city I should visit next. I make it a game. I ask for the answers to everything I need. The universe never tires of our questions.

I dedicate this chapter to my Turkish soul sisters who took such amazing care of me on that trip. When you ask for help, the support net will appear. Be open to receive it.

Reflection Questions

1. Do you believe in oracles/signs? Are you open to asking for a sign? If so, write your questions down now. If not, explain what your resistance is. What do you have to lose by giving it a try?

2. Think of a time you needed an answer, and it came in the form of a song/book/person/sign. Write down your experience.

3. Was there a time you got a sign or answer and ignored it? What happened when you ignored it?

Get Into Action

Do an experiment. Write down a specific question in your notebook. Here are some examples of questions that are good to start with:

1. Where should I go on my next trip?
2. Which talents do I have that I could use more?
3. Which food do I need to eat more of?
4. Who is a person I should call or contact?

Give the universe a time limit to give you the answer, such as 24-48 hours. Make sure you ask the universe to give you the answer GENTLY. Look and listen for signs and answers on the radio, on street signs, in a magazine, from a stranger sitting next to you, or in your dreams, etc. Write down your results.

Book Recommendation: *E2* by Pam Grout. This book is full of all kinds of ways you can experiment with energy.

CHAPTER 17

Indonesia

LESSON:

Judgment

The year was 1995. I traveled alone by ferry boat to the island of Sumatra, Indonesia and spent one month there. The most vivid memories I have of Sumatra are: the orangutan preserve with mamas swinging with their babies on their backs, staying in a tree house next to the river and hearing the monkeys howl outside the door, greeting the huge iguanas at breakfast, floating on an innertube down the river for hours, hiking in the hills over Lake Toba and getting lost. Together, with my new-found friends, we walked for hours until we finally found a small village with a man who drove us back to our hostel. Thank you, travel angels.

Indonesia is a nation made of many islands. Each island is

different and has different customs and traditions. On the island of Sumatra, the area around Lake Toba is Christian. And the city on the tip, Banda Aceh, is a Muslim city. At that time, it was well-known as a militant part of Indonesia, and Western tourists were discouraged from going there.

To get to the island of Pulau Weh, you need to take the ferry boat from Banda Aceh. It was my first visit to a Muslim city. I wore pants and long sleeves and covered my hair out of respect for the traditions of the locals. That is one thing I have learned as a traveler: "When in Rome, do as the Romans do."

So, there I was, wandering around the city of Banda Aceh. I went into the shops and smiled at the shopkeepers. My experience in Indonesia—and the world—is that most people are friendly. One woman struck up a conversation with me. She knew a little English. We chatted about children. We laughed about something we had in common.

Then she asked me, "Which country are you from?" and I replied, "I am American." Her face completely changed. Her expression grew dark, and she immediately turned and walked away.

I was dumbstruck. It was the first-time in my life that someone had acted so rudely to me based solely on my nationality. Now I had heard my share of jokes about the "dumb Americans" and the "ugly American tourist". I usually took it in stride. This was different. This woman actually looked at me with HATE in her eyes.

Understand that at the time I was in Indonesia, the First Gulf War had just ended a few years before. There were ongoing conflicts in the Middle East between the U.S. Government and Muslim fundamentalists. A lot of rhetoric of fear and hate was being spouted in the media. I felt angry for being judged because of the policies and politics of my country; especially since I was not in favor of those policies, nor did I vote for them.

What I really want to convey here is that I am a traveler. I went to Indonesia to experience the culture there, not to change or judge it. It is because I have traveled so much that I am much more tolerant. I believe that traveling brings more peace to the world by building friendships and mutual understanding.

On that day, in Banda Aceh, before I divulged the country of my passport, we were just two women laughing and chatting about kids. The look on that woman's face is etched in my mind as a reminder of how political differences can infect the human condition like a disease. When we look at how we are different, we will find evidence. But if we look how we are the same, we will find more evidence and more peace.

It is interesting to note that Indonesia itself is a good example of this. There are Christian, Muslim, and Buddhist enclaves throughout the islands, and yet, the people are all part of one country. On the island of Bali, the Balinese people place paramount importance on keeping in balance. This is quite possibly what has maintained the peace in such a diverse country. I have heard that the natives of each island do not particularly like each other or mix much, but they do maintain peace.

Lesson: I don't have to agree with you for us to be friends.

Reflection Questions

1. How do these lessons apply to your life?

2. Have you ever judged someone from another country because their ways are different from yours? Which country?

3. How well do you interact with people who are "different" from you? How many friends do you have who are Asian/Hispanic/Black/Muslim/Jewish/Caucasian/Gay/Pacific Islander/Native American, etc.?

4. If this chapter is making you uncomfortable, ask yourself why. Did you have a negative experience with a specific person that made you feel the way you do, or did you gain your perspective from the media/family?

Get Into Action

Choose a group of people with whom you have little or no interaction or experience with. Make it your goal to befriend at least one person from that ethnic group. Do this by joining a club or interacting with them online. Your goal in this activity is to find out how much you have in common.

CHAPTER 18

Cuba

LESSON:

Be Grateful for Your Freedoms

In 2000, I was teaching Spanish in a public high school in Los Angeles. That year, I spent my summer vacation traveling through Mexico and Cuba. Because of the U.S. Embargo on travel and trade to Cuba, I flew from Cancun, Mexico over to Havana with a special educator visa on a group study program with the non-profit organization called Global Exchange.

I spent three weeks in Havana, studying Afro-Cuban dance, percussion and salsa dancing. It was August, and all of Havana was celebrating Carnival along the Malecón. The streets of Havana were filled with music, colorful murals, and paintings of Che Guevara. Fidel Castro had been in power for almost fifty years.

What surprised me most about Cuba were the sharp contrasts of darkness and light. For example, there were supermarkets filled with items, but only foreigners were allowed to enter. Many locales only accepted U.S. dollars, not Cuban pesos. A glass of rum cost about fifty cents, whereas bottled water was about four U.S. dollars. Having a telephone was a super luxury. Moreover, most Cubans were not allowed to talk to foreigners unless they had a specific job in tourism. If they were caught speaking to a foreigner, they could be put in jail. (1) Medical care was free under the socialized system, but some types of medicine and medical equipment were hard to come by and very expensive because of the embargo. There was a VAST difference between the experience of the average Cuban citizen and the foreigners who lived there. The electricity in Havana went out every day for a few minutes, and Cubans were absolutely NOT allowed to make any complaints or protest against the government.

In contrast to the harsh living conditions, Cubans have their music. Music is heard on every street corner all day long. I have never danced as much as I did in Cuba. Our dance classes started early and lasted for three hours. Then we took a break for lunch. Afternoon salsa clubs opened around four p.m. Then late-night music played from about ten p.m. until three or four a.m. Our ritual was to dance in the morning, have lunch, take a siesta (nap), then dance until very late. Around three or four a.m. you could always find people out on the terrace of our hotel, smoking cigars, drinking some rum, and playing dominoes.

It surprised me that in a place with limited freedom and resources, most people were genuinely happy. Since I speak

Spanish fluently and could pass for a Cuban, I went into several Cuban friends' homes. This, of course, put them in jeopardy with the police, but they were enormously generous and curious. They cooked a big meal for me, with food that was difficult to find in Cuban markets, and asked me millions of questions.

The big question was, "What is the rest of the world like?" Most Cubans did not have a passport to leave the country. Very few people were allowed to travel at all. If you were lucky enough to get a visa to travel, you had to leave your spouse and/or children behind to make sure you returned. Imagine what it would feel like if you did not have the freedom to leave your city or country?

This trip highlighted for me just how blessed I was. In Cuba, at that time, the only access to information about the outside world was through the media channels, which were most definitely censored. The Cubans wanted to hear my stories of the world. One woman I met, Annabella*, had a beautiful daughter named Ariel*, aged ten. They were both so kind and wonderful to me. I spent as much time with them as I could. Annabella was planning to send her daughter to live in Miami with her father if she could get a visa, knowing full well that once Ariel left, they would probably never see each other again. I cried when I heard their story. They both came to see me off when I left. I do not know where they are now, but I pray that they are well and that their situation has improved since the embargo was lifted.

The two greatest lessons I learned in Cuba were to be profoundly grateful for what I have and to know that it is not our circumstances which define us. Even if the government denied the people their freedom, they still danced, laughed, and played music every day. Finding joy in the simple pleasures of life.

Nelson Mandela, from his jail cell where he was imprisoned unjustly for twenty-seven years, said that this line from William Earnest Henley's poem Invictus, was his lifeline in moments of despair:

"I am the master of my fate, I am the captain of my soul."

No one can take away the power of your thoughts unless you let them.

Reflection Questions

1. Where do you lack freedom in your life? Is there something which you obsess over or feel controlled by? Maybe a boss, a parent, a teacher, or an addiction? Maybe you feel you must have that one "thing" or "person" in order to be happy? How is this "thing" controlling you?

2. How would your life be different if you could not travel outside your country? How would you feel if you were separated from your family members never to see them again?

3. What do you take for granted that some people on the planet do not have, such as clean water? Electricity? A telephone/car? A college education? Parents who are still married or still alive?

4. Think of someone in your past that you met on a trip or at school that you felt incredibly close to then never saw again. What was it about that interaction that had such an effect on you?

Get Into Action

Choose one area of your life where you feel the least freedom. Take at least one action this week to regain your power. Write down how it feels to be more empowered.

For example, in my case, I used to sing a lot in live performances, but I shut down my voice and gave away my power to some bullies in middle school. Recently, I have been taking voice lessons and singing again to build up my voice and regain my freedom of expression.

CHAPTER 19

The Vatican

LESSON:

The Power of Compound Interest

"Compound Interest is the eighth greatest wonder of the world." -A. Einstein

The first time I went to Saint Peter's Square to see the Sistine Chapel was in 1987.

Vatican City, in the middle of Rome, Italy, is the smallest country in the world, and yet, it is one of the wealthiest. It has its own governing body, its own postal system, and even had its own currency, the Vatican Lire, until 2000. (1)

The Vatican is the center of the Roman Catholic religion, practiced by millions of people around the globe. I am not here to advocate for or against Catholicism. My point is how did an entity so tiny in size amass so much wealth and power?

One seed, over time, grows into a forest.

The Catholic Popes, for centuries, planted seeds in the minds of people and carefully watered and tended to those seeds. Those seeds were made of certain religious tenets.

They amassed wealth by owning land. If you go to Italy, France, Spain, Portugal, Mexico, or South America, you will find some of the most valuable real estate is owned by the Catholic Church. All those sprawling cathedrals in the center of town are all owned by one of the largest real estate conglomerates in the world, the Vatican. (2)

Land ownership is a perfect example of the value of compound interest. What do you think a square foot of land is now worth in downtown Rome? Millions. Now multiply that by hundreds of cathedrals worldwide. Then, on top of that figure, add the value of all the precious works of art housed in those cathedrals and the Vatican's gold reserves. It is virtually impossible to quantify the exact value. Suffice to say, it is MASSIVE. (3)

I could go on and speak of the stock that the Vatican owns in certain lucrative companies, but you get the point.

One small group, over centuries, has amassed one of the largest stocks of wealth known in history. Does it matter that the country itself is less than two miles wide?

No.

Clearly, in this instance, size does not matter. I am tempted to throw in a David and Goliath reference here.

One final, important demonstration of the power of compound interest is the Sistine Chapel itself, painted by Michelangelo over the course of four years. One man, so devoted to his craft, was willing to dedicate a portion of his life lying on his back, in an excruciating position, painting the most intricate and minute details. If you go to see the Sistine Chapel's ceiling, you will understand viscerally just how powerful concentrated effort over time can be.

It's so powerful, in fact, that one river cut through the Grand Canyon to create the seventh wonder of the world.

Isn't is perfect that Albert Einstein called compound interest the eighth wonder of the world?

Reflection Questions

1. In which area of your life are you willing to put in the time and effort to use the principle of compound interest in your favor?

2. How much money do you save each month? Most investors recommend saving or investing at least ten percent of your monthly income. Do you have a savings account? An investment account? A 401K? Are you planning for your retirement?

3. What unnecessary items do you spend a lot of money on? For example, could you give up your Starbucks coffee and make coffee at home, or better yet, quit drinking coffee altogether?

Get Into Action

Step 1: Do a 30-day challenge to save money. Choose one specific thing you would like to save the money for. Set the amount you need to save for this item and budget accordingly. Reward yourself when you reach your savings goal.

Step 2: Set up a savings/retirement/investment account if you do not have one already. Most large banks have staff members who can advise you on how to do this.

CHAPTER 20

Rwanda

LESSON:

The Effects of War

In December 2010, after leaving Uganda, I crossed the border into Rwanda. My goal was to investigate the possibility of helping to build a school for orphans there. My friend, Jamie Bianchini of www.peacepedalers.com, had met a man named Pierre* on his travels through Rwanda and put me in contact with him. I met Pierre at the border and stayed with him and his wife for one week.

Pierre, like most of the people in Rwanda, was profoundly affected by the tribal war and genocide of the Tutsi peoples in 1994. (1) As a young boy, he watched as his entire family was murdered before his eyes. He survived by running and hiding in a bush and foraging for food. Later, he was found and adopted by an elderly woman who sent him to school. His dream was to start his own school for orphans in Kigali, the capital city.

After getting to know Pierre and spending a week living in his home, I could see how much the war had affected his personality. He was educated, but in so many ways, he still acted like that small child fighting for survival. After looking over his business plan and watching him closely, I was not convinced that he was ready to be the administrator of a school. So, I gave him a job at the school I helped build in Uganda. I paid for his room and board and a teaching salary. I wanted him to gain some experience before investing the large sum of money it would take to build a school in Rwanda.

Unfortunately, Pierre had other plans. Once he arrived in Uganda, he started making demands and expecting special treatment. This did not go over well with me or with the headmaster of the school, who is a dear friend of mine. After about one week, Pierre took the money and left for Rwanda without so much as a goodbye to his hosts.

Over the years, I still get messages from Pierre. He has recently rented a space and has started a small school there. Soon, he will break ground to expand the school. I hope that time has been his teacher and he has learned to be more responsible. I wish him good luck and Godspeed.

May the memory of that kind woman who saved him transmute and burn away his dark memories of the war.

What I know beyond a shadow of a doubt is that war and death create an energetic residue which remains long after the war is over. It lives in the cellular memory and the subconscious minds of the people who suffered. (2)

Pierre told me that after the war in Rwanda ended, the government decreed that no one was allowed to speak of it ever. I do not know if this is true or not. What I do know from all of my experience and research is that trauma, if not healed or expressed, goes underground. Turned within, it can cause illness, depression, or aggression. Post-Traumatic Stress Disorder is common among people who have lived in a war zone; there is no exact cure and it may take years to heal. (3)

Everywhere I went in Rwanda, I was greeted as a "foreign" person, called "Omozuno". The children would beg, "Gimme money." That was all they knew of foreigners who came after the war to distribute food and funds. Foreigners who showed up, bearing gifts, and then left, much like the colonists before them. But what those government organizations sent after the war did not address were the emotional scars and underlying tribal issues which caused the war.

Twenty-four years have passed since those tragic events, and the people of Rwanda have slowly rebuilt their homes and families. I have not been back since 2010, but based on my communications with Pierre and other friends who have visited, I hear that things are improving. Humans are amazingly resilient, but it takes time to heal a wound. Bureaucracies and societal norms change slowly. Being in a war zone or close to one is a terrible shock to the system on a physical, emotional, and psychic level.

In our ordinary, everyday lives, we take for granted that common decency will be honored. During war, all those "agreements" are tossed out the window. The stability we base so much on is revealed to be not stable at all. On the one hand, it is scary; on the other hand, it teaches an incredibly valuable lesson that stability is an internal phenomenon.

I create my own sense of stability. If I expect the rest of the word to follow my plan, I will be knocked down and disappointed. In times of war, great tragedies occur, but so do incredible acts of kindness and heroism. Everything is extreme and intensified.

As the saying goes, "Do not judge a man until you walk in his shoes." I say a prayer that new life emerges in Rwanda. Like the lotus flower growing in the mud, even in the darkest time, there is collateral beauty.

Reflection Questions

1. Think of the hardest or darkest time in your life. What lessons did it teach you? What skill did you learn to survive that helps you now? How did that experience shape who you are now?

2. Have you ever been in a war zone? Do you know anyone who has? How were you or they affected emotionally by the experience? Even if it was long ago, what behavioral traits do you or they still exhibit today that are signs of having lived that experience? (PTSD is a good example of this. It can be triggered by events happening much later.)

3. Were your parents or grandparents alive during WWII? What behaviors and values do they have which are different from the values of today? What fears do they have which they passed on to you, consciously or unconsciously?

4. Do you or anyone you know have a history of abando
or loss? How does it affect the choices you or they mak
What are some ways you or they could use this experie
help others?

Get Into Action

Visit a local center for immigrants or an orphanage and
volunteer your time/clothes/food/expertise to help someone.
What we give to others, we give to ourselves. Every time I
volunteer, I come away feeling very good afterwards. There
is something about helping others that takes our focus off
our own problems and helps us see that there are others with
far bigger issues to solve. At the very least, just seeing how
grateful and appreciative someone is for your help will uplift
your spirits.

Movie Recommendation: Watch the movie *Collateral
Beauty* to see how beautiful miracles can come from great
tragedy.

Book Recommendation: *The Biology of Belief* by Bruce
Lipton to learn more about how our thoughts and experiences
affect our cells.

CHAPTER 21

France

LESSON:

It's a Small World After All

In the summer of 1992, I went to the South of France for one month to learn French in a small town called Hyeres, near Marseille.

I went alone.

The very first day I arrived, I called my boyfriend in Italy from a phone booth, full of doubts and fears.

"What if I don't make any friends? What if no one likes me?" I cried.

I remember this moment like it is etched in stone. He laughed and said, "Everywhere you go, you make friends. Why would it be any different now?"

He was right. I had traveled and moved many times, and in each new place, I had made many friends. Why was I so scared? It's funny the way the mind plays tricks on us. The ego is keen to keep our focus on what is missing, wrong, or lacking. When we get scared, we suddenly forget all the times we have been successful. Watch this tendency in yourself the next time you go somewhere or try something new.

The first day I moved in, most of the students had not arrived yet, so the dormitory was empty. So, I headed over to the commissary to eat. You know that feeling, like the first day at a new school? People are sitting in pairs or groups, looking like they have known each other for years, and your stomach sinks...

That's how I felt. Plus, I did not know how to speak any French yet, so I felt even more like a fish out of water.

I went over to get a tray of food, and a sound like thunder boomed from across the very large room. I heard a voice yell, "Ooh, Micaela!" I was so surprised, I jumped. I did not know a soul there, so how would anyone know my name?

I looked across the tables and saw an Italian man named Tommaso calling to me.

What are the odds that, in that dining commons in a very small French town, I would run into someone I knew? Very slim, right? When you consider that I met Tommaso in 1986, while I was walking through the streets of Florence seven years before, the odds get even slimmer.

This all on the same day that I called my boyfriend in tears in fear that I might not make any friends.

The universe works in miraculous ways and the world is not as big as we think. Over the years, I have run into people I know in the strangest places.

Needless to say, I made many wonderful new friends in my classes and had a lovely time that summer. We even had some great adventures, which I will elaborate on more in the chapter on Monaco.

Ask for friends, and they will show up. Be open, be ready. And don't let that pesky ego get you down, okay?

Reflection Questions

1. When in your life have you had a synchronistic event happen, where you were at the right place at the right time?

2. Think of a time you had to do or go somewhere new. How did you feel on the first day? What were you afraid of? How did the day go?

3. Think of an area of your life where you have little or no confidence. Then make a list of where and when you have done something similar with success. Use this new information to try something new or take the next step.

4. Have you ever studied a new language? Have you visited a country where that language is spoken? Which language would you love to learn? What is stopping you from learning it? Are there people in your city who speak that language? Are you willing to take a class or read a book to learn? Why or why not?

Get Into Action

Choose a language you would like to learn. Enroll in a class or exchange program this week to start learning. Find someone who speaks that language in your city or online and offer to trade lessons to teach them something you know.

And if you are ever feeling down, take a trip to Disneyland to go on the Small World ride. Sing the song. No matter how many times I go, I am always filled with wonder and joy at the magic there.

CHAPTER 22

Vietnam

LESSON:

Resiliency

The year was 2001. I spent one month in Vietnam, traveling from Saigon all the way up to the northern border with China, to a small town called Sa Pa. Sa Pa was by far my favorite place in Vietnam, nestled high in the hills, surrounded by misty clouds and rice fields. It is a sharp contrast from the hustle and bustle of Hanoi.

It was hard for me to be in Vietnam—and not because it is not beautiful. There are gorgeous beaches and incredible food. It was hard because everywhere I went I saw reminders of the Vietnam War. Although I was a small child when this war occurred, there was part of me that felt a terrible sense of guilt or remorse for the damage done there by a country which I call home.

Many tourists visit the Cu Chi District in Ho Chi Mihn City (Hanoi), where you can walk through the underground tunnels that the Vietcong built to travel and send messages under the United States' lines of defense. What is incredible about these tunnels is how vast and small they are. There are tens of thousands of tunnels, circa fifteen feet deep and 250 KM (155 Miles) long. (1) I am in awe of the persistence and focus it must have taken for those soldiers to build that network. Sometimes, they dug with their bare hands.

Some of you might know or be someone who fought in the Vietnam War. Some men were "drafted" (obliged by the government) and some volunteered, and some men fled to Canada and Mexico to evade the draft. I do not wish to condemn anyone for their choices. No matter what side we choose in battle, there are always consequences. In war, people are capable of both atrocious acts and incredible bravery. That is what it means to be human. We have a light and dark side.

When I taught at university, we often debated the pros and cons of the death penalty. When the students asked me where I stood on this issue, this was my reply:

"I personally do not advocate for the killing of any human being. However, if someone killed my children or husband or raped my daughter, I cannot say what I would do. It is easy to judge and point fingers at others, but being in Vietnam taught me to look at myself. Look at my own actions. Where have I been negligent? Where have I been mean or cruel? How have I benefitted from living in a place which may or may not exploit people in other countries? We are all inter-connected. So, no one is immune from being partly to cause for wars that occur on this planet. We are all part of the human condition."

This chapter is on the lesson of resiliency. I went to Vietnam about twenty years after the war was over. I found a country thriving with tourism and new businesses. It seems to me that people always find a way to survive and even thrive after and during hardship, like a small plant that takes root even in granite rock. I am constantly astounded by the resiliency of the human spirit.

Do I wish I could go back and stop the war? Yes.

Do I wish I could stop human suffering? Yes.

Was I treated well as an American traveling in Vietnam? Yes.

Travel shows us things we may not be able to see at home. It shows the impact and consequences of our choices on the rest of the planet.

True peace is when all beings can live in harmony on the planet. Is there more peace now than there was a century ago? Yes. Proportionately, there is.

As much as there are still so many areas where we could be doing more, life is getting better for more and more people on the planet. I hope that by writing, I can make at least my piece of the world a better place.

Reflection Questions

1. Have you ever been in the military? Do you know anyone who is in the military? How do you feel about members of the armed forces? Do you have a positive view or a negative one?

2. Would you be willing to fight for your country if you were obliged by the government to do so? Or would you move to another country?

3. Is military service mandatory in your country? What are your thoughts on disbanding the military in your country? Is your country "protected" by another country's military forces? And how do you feel about that? Would you be willing to serve instead?

4. Have you ever been the victim of abuse or serious crime? What emotions did you feel toward your assailants? Do you think you could harm them out of revenge or vindication?

5. What are some alternatives to having an army? How can we create a world in the future without weapons?

6. Have you ever been in jail or imprisoned? Do you know someone who has? How are they similar or dissimilar to you?

7. Have you ever broken the law? Be honest here; even speeding on the freeway technically is breaking the law. If you did, what excuse did you tell yourself to make it okay? Which crimes are minor, in your opinion, and which are not?

Get Into Action

Look at one area of your life where you have or are tempted to break a rule or law, such as: driving, paying your taxes, stealing, lying, or hurting an animal or person. (No one is going to see this except for you.) Ask yourself, if everyone did what you are doing, what would happen? Write down your answers. Ask yourself how many times you have done one or more of these things in your lifetime. Write down the number. Does looking at these answers change your view of who or what a criminal looks like? And should you or should you not pay a penalty for these actions? Who is the judge? Make a vow to change your behavior in at least one area where it is adversely affecting others.

CHAPTER 23
South Korea

LESSON:

Work Smarter, Not Harder

In 2001, my boyfriend, who was also a teacher, and I flew to Seoul, Korea to teach English at a summer camp at the University of Suwon.

I need to backtrack a little first for this to make sense. From 1998 to 2001, I taught at a public high school in Los Angeles. (I learned so many lessons from that experience that it may deserve its own book.) I had two hundred teenage students per day. Being a public school teacher in the U.S., unfortunately, is not a highly paid position, even though I had a B.A. and a master's degree. I made $40,000 in my first year. For some of you, that may seem like a lot of money, but in Los Angeles, it is most definitely not. The days were long, and I went to school at night to complete my teaching credential and my second master's degree. Most days, I left the house at about eight a.m. and returned home at midnight.

At that time in my life, there were many things that wore me down emotionally, and I had chronic pain in my neck. I got to the point where I couldn't move my neck without muscle relaxants. My body was clearly sending me a message. Thank goodness, I listened. I decided to leave my tenured position and take a year off from teaching to travel.

My boyfriend was a first-year teacher with big student loans to pay off. Does this sound familiar to any of you?

The big question was, how could we travel around the world for one year and find a way to pay for it?

I asked him, "If I can find a way to pay for it, will you come with me?" He said, "Yes, of course."

First, I asked the universe for help. And then I started asking my friends. About a week later, my friend gave me this flyer she got from one of her students about a job teaching in Korea for one month. The salary was good, and all expenses were paid. They were even going to pay for one-way airfare to get to Korea. Right away, we said, "YES."

I sold my car, gave away my furniture, put my clothes into storage, and bought a Circle Asia Flight Pass. This is a special kind of ticket sold by airline consolidators which allows the traveler to make five stops in different cities and is valid for one year.

When we arrived in Korea, we were welcomed by a staff member who took us to our new lodgings. I am not exaggerating when I say that we stayed in a five-star hotel next to the university campus. All our meals were included. For four weeks, we taught English to bright, eager, elementary-aged students and went on various field trips with them. After the malaise of teenagers, these eager beavers so full of enthusiasm were a welcome respite.

At the end of the four weeks, we were paid in cash with enough money to pay for six months of travel in Southeast Asia. Traveling in Asia as a backpacker is quite inexpensive. For example, in the twelve months we traveled to thirteen countries, we spent a total of five thousand U.S. dollars. It was 2001, so now that would be about eight to ten thousand dollars. Still, compared to what it costs me to live in Los Angeles, that's a steal.

We had such a good experience in Korea that we went back in the winter and taught another one-month course, which paid for the rest of our trip.

So many times, I have heard people say, "I would love to travel to _____, but I don't have the money." In my experience, it is NOT the money which holds us back. It is the fear of giving up our safety net.

I had faith when I gave up my tenured position that I would and could find another job teaching. I had to believe in myself and my abilities and trust the universe. As an aside, I should add that when I returned home, I did, indeed, get a new position on the first day I applied.

The moral of this story is TRUST. Trust that you are good at what you do. Do it with passion. I love to teach. And after over twenty-five years of doing it, I can say without blushing that I am good at it.

It is not about how many hours you work. It is about HOW you work. When you love what you do, the money will always follow. I found a way to teach all over the world and get paid well to do it.

It does not matter what your education is, although in my profession, it helps. If you love to sing, SING. If you love to build, BUILD.

Ask the universe for help. Ask friends for leads. Be open to go somewhere new. There may be a great demand for your skill set in another place. GO.

Don't work hard. Working hard makes us tired and sick. Work smarter.

Reflection Questions

1. On a scale of 1-10, how much do you love your job? If the score is less than 6, what job would you like to do more? What is stopping you from changing jobs?

2. What are some ways you could earn extra income by doing what you love?

3. What are you putting off because you are waiting for the "right" time or offer? What if that right time never comes? Are you willing to give up on this dream?

4. What do you have in your house that you no longer use or need? Could you sell it or donate it for a tax break or give it to someone who needs it?

Get Into Action

1. Choose one job you have always wanted to try but are not currently doing. Look up where there is a college or program teaching more about it. See if you can take some time off from your job or go at night to take some classes. Some companies encourage their employees to increase their skillset and will help pay for your fees. Ask the Human Resources Department where you work.

2. Declutter your home or garage. You would be surprised at how liberating it feels to give stuff away or sell it.

3. If you are interested in teaching English abroad, go to www.daveseslcafe.com to peruse the listings for jobs around the world.

CHAPTER 24

Scotland

LESSON:

Forgiveness

> *"Love can only survive when our wounds are acknowledged and healed."*
> -Brene Brown

In 1990, I flew to England with my mother and my grandmother. We took the train up to Glasgow to tour Scotland. It was October, and the leaves were changing. What beautiful countryside and colors.

One of the most memorable things we did on that trip was to visit Loch Ness, home to the infamous Loch Ness monster. No one has seen it, but almost everyone who has been to Scotland has heard of it. It is one of those mysteries on the planet.

Let's talk about those things we cannot see, and yet, they still affect us. My grandmother's family came over from England. However, my mother was adopted as a baby. The only thing I know about her biological mother is that she was Scottish. So, somewhere in Scotland, I may have aunties, uncles, and cousins. Even though I have never met my biological grandmother, her presence has been felt keenly in direct and indirect ways.

I can say from personal experience and from the years I worked one-on-one with clients as a personal coach/healer that major childhood traumas are stored in the body as blocked energy. We must choose to heal them and release them, or they stay in our body and cause disease and may even be passed on to our children. As a certified hypnotherapist, I studied the intricate connection between the mother and the fetus. What the mother feels, the baby feels. (1) All of it. And the parents' trauma is also transferred to the child's DNA via cellular memory. (2) In fact, Native American tribes believe that we inherit up to seven generations of memories. Seven generations! (3)(4) Recent science experiments are showing that it may be even more. (5)

I do not know what it is like to be physically abandoned by my mother or father. But I do know for sure that some people are not ready or even capable of being good parents. Is it better to not have a child you are not ready to take of, to keep the child, or to give it away to an orphanage? I will let you make your own choice here because it is a very personal choice.

No matter what we decide, there are consequences to each decision. My biological grandmother chose to give her baby up for adoption. I believe that my mother always carried that knowledge in her heart as a wound. Although my adoptive grandmother raised my mother to the best of her ability, they were never very close. I have compassion for my biological grandmother and my mother. They both experienced being pregnant, alone, and afraid. I, too, know what this feels like, and it is difficult and heart-wrenching. No matter which path one chooses, the choice is painful, and the baby will be affected adversely.

Destructive family patterns such as abandonment, sexual abuse, alcoholism, and drug addictions can and will keep on repeating over and over in future generations unless the deep emotional wounds are healed. (6) I did decades of therapy, seminars, holistic healing, and self-hypnosis to heal myself. Dysfunctional patterns are difficult to break because they are hard-wired in the brain. Freud called it "Repetition Compulsion". (7) In order to change, we must create a whole new belief system. And sometimes, that requires acting in ways that go against the status quo. When push comes to shove, you must choose if you want to be healed or if you want to keep everyone feeling comfortable around you.

I, like many people, held resentments and anger toward my parents. I confronted them directly on some of the ways I felt that they could or should have done better. My father, in his later years, wrote a long letter of apology to me, God rest his soul. Apologies soothe the pain, but don't hold your breath to get one. Parents are human, and humans have an uncanny stubborn streak when it comes to admitting their own mistakes. My parents have/had scars too. I see their wounds and the little child in them who longs to be loved. I see how they could never give me what they never received or learned themselves.

Forgiveness is a miraculous thing. It does not mean that you condone or agree with whatever wrongs happened. It just allows you to have more freedom to move forward, instead of staying stuck in the blame game. Forgive and let go. Forgive and let go. Forgive and let go. Even if you have to keep doing it a thousand times.

This is your life. Once you are an adult, you get to make your own choices of who you spend time with or not. No one has power over you unless you give it away to them. It took me many years to take back my power, but once I did, I felt an enormous sense of freedom.

I am grateful for the lessons I learned from my parents and my grandparents. Whether good or bad, painful or ugly, I am who I am today because of the experiences I have lived. From the hardships and trauma I endured, I became stronger, more self-reliant, and much more discerning as to who and where I give my time and my energy.

Isn't it time to just let that s**t go?

Reflection Questions

1. Do you feel angry/resentful/betrayed/disappointed in your mother? Your father? Is there something they have done or said that you carry around as a burden? Are you willing to forgive them? This does not mean you condone their actions. It simply means you are willing to free yourself from the past.

2. Can you see the "wounded child" in your parents? Yes or no? Did they experience abuse or trauma as children which still affects them today?

3. Do you have any family members you have never met? Where are they? Write their names and locations. Would you like to meet them? If so, when will you go? If no, why not? There is no judgment on whichever you decide. These are open-ended questions just to look deeper into your own motivations.

4. Which patterns do you see in your family which have been passed on? Are these patterns helpful or hurtful? Make a list of any family patterns you wish to change. Get into action to create new habits.

5. Have you ever been estranged or separated from family members because of quarrels, feuds, or abandonment? How does this affect you? Are any of your family members toxic or abusive? Are you better off not having any interaction with them? There is no right or wrong answer.

Get Into Action

1. Take A DNA test to find family members you have never met, especially if you or your parents were adopted.

In 2018, I took a DNA test to find out more about my biological grandparents. I was surprised to discover that while, yes, I do have some ancestry from Scotland, I also have cousins who live in Sweden. With the advent of DNA testing being easily available and affordable, there are many stories of family members reunited after decades of separation. Some of these stories have happy endings, some not. But there is always a sense of closure.

2. Go to Colin Tipping's website, www.radicalforgiveness.com, which has a Forgiveness Worksheet. This process will help you work through feelings of anger/resentment/abandonment.

I have completed the worksheet many times. It is very transformational.

Choose a family member or friend you have negative feelings toward to complete the Forgiveness Worksheet. Repeat the process every time you feel anger or resentment come up.

Movie Recommendations: Two of the best movies I have ever seen on forgiveness are:

The Shack by William P. Young
Five People You Meet in Heaven by Mitch Albom

Every time I watch these movies, I cry buckets of tears. They have helped me understand that there is much more to our lives than what we see on the surface.

Book Recommendation: Brene Brown's *The Gifts of Imperfection: Let Go of Who You Think You're Supposed to Be and Embrace Who You Are*

CHAPTER 25

Andorra

LESSON:

Read the Fine Print

First, how many of you know where Andorra is? Quick, go find it on a map.

Andorra is a small country in the North of Spain, near the Pyrenees Mountains.

In spring of 1989, I was about to complete my year-long study abroad program in Madrid and was looking for ways to make money to travel around Europe on a Eurail Pass.

One day, while walking to school, I happened upon a small travel agency offering various study and work programs. I asked about any jobs teaching English in Spain over the summer. The agent showed me this beautiful brochure of a camp in the Pyrenees mountains, near Andorra. We would be camp counselors for four weeks for well-behaved, elementary-aged children. Sounded perfect, right?

"Sounded" is the operative word.

I was so excited, I convinced my friend Mary to come along too, so that afterwards we could travel together.

Well, this was one of those times I learned a lesson the HARD way. I looked at the pictures and did not read the fine print in the contract.

Off we went—tra-la-la.

We took a bus to the town where the camp was, expecting to see green trees and flowing rivers.

Lo and behold, we arrived in what appeared to be a dry, deserted school in the middle of nowhere.

This was not Andorra, Toto!

The school did, indeed, have many enthusiastic children, although "well-behaved" was a stretch. The program director was an older man who spent most days very drunk in his office. There was no curriculum and no supervision. I am not exaggerating.

Those parents who sent their beloved children off to learn English got snowed. And we, the eager English teachers, were left high and dry, to our own devices. Most of the teachers were good-hearted and did their best to teach with what few resources they had. But some were just there to get paid and sat on their butts all day.

Looking back now, it was like a comedy of errors. We had many laughs, Melanie and I and those kids.

It was about ninety-plus degrees Fahrenheit every day, so the only thing we could do was spend most of the time in the pool. Most of the students were more than happy NOT to speak English since it was their parents' idea to come to camp and not theirs. In class, they preferred just asking me questions about life. I would answer them back in English and Spanish, so hopefully, they did learn something useful.

Here's a heads-up about life. If someone makes you an offer that sounds too good to be true or shows you a pretty photo on their Tinder dating profile, READ the small print. Ask questions. Find out what you are really getting into before saying "YES".

Reflection Questions

1. Have you ever said "YES" to something and then later found out it was not what you expected? What did you learn from this experience?

2. When life gives you lemons, what do you do? Make lemonade or give up?

3. Think of the last time you went somewhere completely new? How long ago was it? The last time you ordered something brand new at a restaurant? On a scale of 1-10, how much of a creature of habit are you? How could you be more spontaneous? What areas of your life could use more spontaneity?

Get Into Action

(This one is fun!)

Get out a big map of the world or of your country or city and lay it out in front of you. Close your eyes—no peeking! Move your arm in circles in the air and then put your finger down on one spot. Now go and visit that place this weekend or this month. No cheating and switching to another place. Go on a spontaneous adventure somewhere new. Be open to the synchronicities and miracles. Write down what happens.

Singing with the children at the Good Hope School, Uganda, Africa. 2009

Celebrating my Italian heritage in Rome, Italy. 2013

Meditating with Buddha in Sokcho, South Korea. 2003

Petting the kangaroos in Sydney, Australia. 2003

Exploring the highlands at Lake Bunyonyi, Uganda, Africa. 2009

Visiting Butchart Gardens with my grandmother, Victoria, Canada. 1993

Feeding the elephants in Chiang Mai, Thailand. 1995

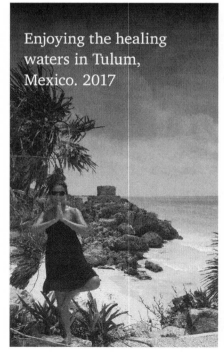

Enjoying the healing waters in Tulum, Mexico. 2017

Wearing a traditional yukata for the Summer Flower Festival in Tokyo, Japan. 1994

My father
looking dapper in
Kamakura, Japan.
Circa 1960.

Cheering at
the Olympics
in Barcelona,
Spain. 1992

Witnessing the magic and
miracles in Glastonbury,
England. 2017

Contemplating art
and freedom in
Havana, Cuba. 2000

Enjoying the
blessings with my
husband, Hawaii,
USA. 2017

Feeling empowered at the
Parthenon in Athens, Greece. 1989

CHAPTER 26

Holland

LESSON:

People Show You Who They Are

The year was 2003. I flew from Seoul, Korea to Amsterdam to meet a man I had a huge crush on.

First, let me explain why I flew halfway across the globe to meet someone I had only spent a total of ten hours with in my entire life. Let's go back to the year before.

In July of 2002, I boarded a train from Montreal, Canada to New York City. I had been up in Montreal for two weeks, taking a refresher course in French and visiting some friends. The day I got to the train station, I was waiting in line, and next to me was a man. I was tired since I had been up all night celebrating and had a raging headache. So, my head was down.

I glanced over and noticed his shoes—brown, worn cowboy boots. I have a thing for shoes. If I like your shoes, I will like you. I recall thinking, cool shoes.

So, I boarded the train to find my assigned seat. For those of you who have been on a train or a plane, admit it; in your head, you say to yourself, I hope that I get to sit next to that guy/girl. Or the opposite, which is also quite common—Lord, please don't sit me next to that person!

I got to my seat, and as fate would have it, my wish was granted. The handsome man with the cool shoes was sitting right next to me.

His name was Jose'*, and he was English and Portuguese. We hit it off immediately and spent the whole trip laughing and flirting outrageously. He did mention that he was living with a woman at the time, but somehow, my ego put that important piece of information in a deep, dark corner easy to be ignored. What was the harm, I thought? After we got to our destination, we would never see each other again. Besides, we were just joking around. Nothing physical transpired.

He gave me his email address and asked me to write if I was ever in his city.

That was in July 2002. Later that year, in September, I flew to Korea. I got a new teaching contract in Seoul. Seoul is not far from Russia, and it snowed a lot. I was cold and lonely. To add insult to misery, I fractured my toe, so I had to walk around in the snow on crutches. It SUCKED!

In those days, I still was in my "guy-chasing" mode, so I decided to start emailing this man I had met on the train. I felt a big magnetic pull toward him, as if I had met him before. He wrote back and told me he was not happy where he was and was contemplating moving to Portugal to stay with his mother, who was not faring well. We will get to that portion of the story in the chapter on Portugal.

So, let's get back to Holland.

After a disappointing experience in Spain during Christmas, I wrote to Jose'. He said, "Why don't you come and meet me in Holland in the spring for a few weeks?"

Here is the big red flag, a.k.a. life lesson. When people tell you or show you who they are in the very beginning, believe them. Do not let those RED flags go unheeded. I learned this lesson the hard way.

Off I flew, full of wild expectations and romance in my mind. This handsome stranger and I were going to fall madly in love and live happily ever after. Or so the fantasy in my mind went.

I arrived at the Amsterdam airport a bundle of nerves. At first, there was no one waiting for me at the gate, and my heart sunk. Did I make a huge mistake? Was I a fool?

I was just about to burst into tears when there he came, as sexy and cool as I remembered. Oh, I was so relieved and excited.

We boarded the train to Delft, an amazingly beautiful town in the Dutch countryside. I talked too much too fast because I was nervous. And then he kissed me.

You know those times in your life when there is a HUGE build-up to something, and you imagine it and then the real thing does not quite live up to the fantasy. This was NOT one of those times.

This kiss was even better than I had imagined.

We bicycled around windmills and ate picnics of cheese, bread, and wine. It was oh-so-romantic. And I tumbled head over heels in love.

The red flags that I saw, I dismissed immediately. The fact that he stared at all the waitresses, I ignored, even though there was a funny feeling in the pit of my stomach.

And, as always, when you travel with someone, you get to see their best sides and their worst sides. I got to see some of the darker sides.

For example, in Amsterdam, where hashish is legal, he wanted to try all the different kinds of drugs. I was not interested in drugs, but I went along with him to the coffee houses, as they are called. In one shop, the woman who sold him some magic mushrooms advised him to take only a very small bite. That night, while I was sleeping, I was awakened by the horrible sounds of him retching in the bathroom.

"What happened?" I asked. He looked sheepish and said, "I ate the whole mushroom."

So big lesson #2 in Holland: do not over-indulge in the drugs! Jose' spent the whole night worshipping the porcelain god, a polite way of saying vomiting into the toilet all night long. That calamitous night, I went back to bed and I let him work through it on his own. I was thinking, *what an idiot to eat the whole thing!* What I should have been thinking is, *what the heck am I doing with someone who acts this way?*

Oh, but we will get to that big A-HA moment soon.

Holland is a beautiful place to visit; the tulips fields and small towns are gorgeous. Amsterdam is everything you would expect it to be. While I am not condoning the drug trade there, I will say, you get what you ask for. Be careful what you take. Just because something is legal does not mean it is good for you, or that you will feel good in the morning. Catch my drift?

Reflection Questions

1. What are your experiences with drugs or alcohol? Did you ever have a bad experience? What are your thoughts on Holland's liberal policy on drugs? Do you agree or disagree?

2. Have you ever dated or liked someone who was very attractive but not good for you? What lesson did you learn from this interaction?

3. They say that women are attracted to "bad boys". Has this been your experience? What is it about "bad boys" that is like catnip to women?

4. Have you ever flirted or "hooked up" with someone whom you did not know very well, at a party or on vacation? What was the result of this decision?

Get Into Action

Choose one thing you have always secretly wanted to try or do. Within the bounds of legality, is there something you have wanted to try but were afraid it was too risqué, for example, buying sexy lingerie, taking a pole dancing class, or going to a place like Amsterdam? Are you willing to "take a walk on the wild side"?

CHAPTER 27

Portugal

LESSON:

The Importance of Feminine Energy

I had just returned from my trip to Amsterdam in May of 2003. I thought I was madly in love with this man, Jose'*, who although very good-looking and sexy, was obviously not a good match for me. But the attraction was strong, and I did not to pay attention to those red flags. It would take me several more painful experiences to really get this lesson though my thick skull.

He had moved to Portugal to stay with his mother. I was so smitten that I decided that I would fly over to meet him there. Now this is a big red flag, so pay attention.

Let's talk a little bit about the Yin and Yang energies. Yang is the masculine energy. It chases, hunts, plans, and acts. The Yin is the feminine energy. It receives, attracts, and waits patiently.

In this period of my life, I was still in the Yang phase. Like many Western women who are very successful in work and career, I was taught to go out and make things happen! It works well in business, but in relationships, it backfires. Time and time again, I learned this lesson until it was hammered into my brain.

Do not chase the man! Let me repeat this—do not chase the man! Every girlfriend of mine has told me stories of how this behavior has backfired on her. Chasing the man works fine in the beginning. The man is flattered, maybe. He doesn't have to put himself out there and risk rejection. But weeks/months go by, and his interest wanes. His phone calls cease. In short, his motivation is gone. I have experienced this scenario myself too many times to count.

So, there I was, hot to trot to fly to Portugal. I showed up at Jose's house near Lisbon. My first big clue was that he kept telling his mom that we were just "friends". I thought it was because she was a conservative Portuguese woman. But no, it was much more than that.

This was my second visit to Portugal. I had also taken a road trip down the Atlantic coastline back in 1989. It is a beautiful country, full of lazy beach towns and big waves to windsurf. The people are relaxed and warm. In many ways, Portugal reminds me so much of home in California but with fewer people.

Once I arrived at his house, I started to notice all these things that I had refused to see back in Holland. Namely, how much this man liked to drink. How he always had to have a drink. How he did not always tell the truth. How he was selfish and kind of cheap.

But by this point, my blinding sexual attraction had started to wear off.

Years later, in 2011, I had a teacher named Alison Armstrong, who said, "If you meet someone, and your first impression is a 10/10 on the sexual attraction scale, RUN." She said, "RUN away FAST, because you will twist yourself into someone you don't even like just to make this person happy."

I can honestly say that she is right. That is exactly what happened.

You can guess how this story ends already, can't you?

I left Portugal sad and angry, mostly at myself for having been such a fool not to pay attention to the signs sooner. It all came to a head when I found out from Jose's mom that he was still in touch with his former girlfriend back home and that she was patiently waiting for an engagement ring. I don't know if she ever got one. But I can honestly say in hindsight that Jose' was no prize worth waiting for.

The silver lining in this story is that I never chased a man like this again. This was the beginning of the end of that very destructive habit.

It's like the story about drugs. Sometimes, one really bad experience can cure you for good.

Reflection Questions

1. As a woman, do you have more masculine or feminine energy? Be honest here. Do you call men or let them call you? Do you text them to check in to see if they are thinking of you? What are some ways you are acting like the man in your relationships?

2. Men, how does it feel when a woman pursues you? Do you get turned on or off? Do you make less or more effort for her? And if you are in a relationship, what are some ways that you are being less masculine and more inert or passive?

3. In your country, would you say that women are acting more masculine? If yes, why? And are men acting more feminine or androgynous? If so, do you think this is having positive or negative effects on your society?

4. Who is a good example of feminine energy? Are there examples of this in your society? What does that woman do or say which makes you think she is very feminine? Remember, this is about behavior, not how someone dresses. Do you think there are enough feminine leaders or role models? If not, why do you think that is?

Get Into Action

For women: Keep a journal for thirty days. Think about your behavior with the men in your life. Write down ways you act femininely and masculinely. Take notes as to what kinds of responses you are getting from men.

For men: Take notes as to which women you feel attracted to. What qualities do they have that attract you? How do these women act? If you are married or in a relationship, pay attention to your partner's behavior. Does she act receptively toward your actions? Does she receive your gifts and offerings well? Do you feel appreciated? If not, have a conversation with her to explain to her how this makes you feel.

Book Recommendation: The best course I ever took on understanding men was by Alison Armstrong. (www.understandmen.com) She has written many books and courses on how to understand the way men think/speak/fall in love. One of my favorite books by her is called *The Keys to the Kingdom*. She also created a course for men on how to satisfy women. FYI.

SIDE-NOTE

It's important to state for the record that my guardian angels did try to warn me before I left for Portugal. When I went online to buy my plane ticket, I tried four or five times to buy the ticket with my credit card to no avail. The website kept saying, CANNOT PROCESS. My credit card was fine and was working everywhere else with absolutely no problem whatsoever. I got so frustrated, I tried to use a different computer. No luck there either. My angels were sending me a LOUD message. But I was not listening. I ended up going to a travel agent the next day to pay for the ticket. Ironically, because things did not go well in Portugal, I left early. The ticket I bought was non-refundable, so I had to purchase a separate ticket.

Now, when I try to purchase something online or at a store and my credit card does not work for whatever reason, once, twice, I stop. I take it as a sign from the powers that be that this is not the right purchase for me.

If the universe gives you a sign that says DON'T BUY THIS, trust that the angels have your best interest at heart.

CHAPTER 28

Singapore

LESSON:

Clean Out the Clutter

In early 2003, while on our trip around the world, my boyfriend and I took the bus from Thailand through Malaysia, into Singapore. For most of our trip, we had been staying at backpacker hostels. They were cheap and hot, with very thin walls.

We arrived in Singapore late at night, and the only hotel we could find open was much more expensive that what we had been paying. I did not care! I wanted to take a shower and sleep with air conditioning for the first time in month. Remember, Singapore is right on the equator, so the humidity is like one hundred percent. Sweat and mosquitoes are your constant companions. It was nice to take a break from the heat and stay somewhere clean.

That is one thing I can definitely say about Singapore, it is one of the cleanest countries on the planet. Painting graffiti, urinating in elevators, spitting on the sidewalk, not flushing the toilet, and littering are all against the law and subject to a fine, imprisonment or a public caning. Yes, they take cleanliness very seriously, indeed. (1)

One of my favorite hotels is the Raffles Hotel in Singapore, with its old English style, high tea, and the most delicious food imaginable. The buffet has English, Indian, Chinese, and tropical delicacies. The Raffles Hotel is an excellent example of clear, clean, opulent spaces which can be found there.

It's important to note that the entire island of Singapore is only 278 square miles, and yet, its GDP is ranked #4 in the world in terms of population, higher than Kuwait and the UAE! (2)(3) What does that tell you? They must be doing something right. It's like the Switzerland of Asia. Small, clean, and affluent. Singapore also has a large number of immigrants and a large Indian population, who all live together in harmony.

Seventy-six percent of the population in Singapore is of Chinese descent. In China, there is a very ancient tradition of Feng Shui. I learned it when I lived in Asia and still use it in my home and life today. The concept is very simple. Clutter creates blocked energy. Clean, open spaces allow energy to flow.

Singapore is a perfect example of Feng Shui in action. The streets and subways are super-clean. In fact, it was the cleanest public transport system I have ever ridden.

Why do I practice Feng Shui in my own house?

Well, for starters, they have done energy experiments on the correlation between cleanliness and wealth and health.(4)(5) Fascinating, huh? Clean spaces save time, energy, and money.

When I was teaching at university, I used to do an experiment with my students. I asked them to take out their wallets and their notebooks midway into the quarter. I would explain, "I can look at your notebook and how you are keeping your wallet and predict your grades and your relationship with money." They didn't believe me at first, but sure enough, every time, the proof was in the pudding.

T. Harv Eker, one of my teachers on money, says, "How you do one thing is how you do everything." Walk around the streets of Singapore, and you will see what I am referring to. The people there take great pride in their city. Their attention to detail and organization is obvious. And how they keep their city is how they keep their homes and businesses.

The cleaner my wallet, the more money can flow in. The cleaner my body, the healthier I feel. The cleaner my home, the more the energy can flow.

If you are not born with the clean gene, hire someone who will clean your house for you.

Reflection Questions

1. Are you messy or neat? Do you have a garage filled with stuff you do not use? How often do clear out your closet or refrigerator to donate old or expired items?

2. How do you feel when you enter a clean, clear space, such as a large hotel? Do you feel differently? Do you breathe differently? How do you feel when you come home to a messy house? Or to a clean house?

3. Do you think there is a correlation between your space and your money flow? If yes, what are some ways you could create more space and more flow today? If not, look at someone you know who is wealthy and, if possible, visit their home. It is clean or messy?

   Of course, there are exceptions to this rule. You might say, "What about artists or rock stars? They are messy." And yet, how many artists are also broke? And how many rock stars have a cleaning person who cleans their house and an accountant who handles their money?

Get Into Action

Look in your wallet. Is it filled with old receipts and cards that you do not use? Clean it out immediately. Make sure that your wallet is large enough to hold more money. Is it made of nice material, or it is old and falling apart? And look at your desk where you work. Is it cluttered or organized? Every time I clean my desk, I get a new client or a check in the mail. No joke. Try it out.

Book Recommendations: *The Life-Changing Magic of Tidying Up* by Marie Kondo and *Feng Shui for Dummies* by David Daniel Kennedy

SIDE-NOTE

If you are a hoarder or semi-hoarder, de-cluttering might be difficult for you. Hire someone to do it for you, or find a friend who will help you.

CHAPTER 29

Mexico

LESSON:

Transmute Your Pain Into Something Beautiful

*"The cure for anything is saltwater—
tears, sweat, or the sea."*
Isak Dinesen

I've been to Mexico many times over the years. I went on two trips in particular which I will write about as the lessons are intertwined.

The first trip was in 1999. I went to Mexico City to learn and study more about Mexican art and culture. I was very interested in the art of Frida Kahlo and Diego Rivera. I visited Frida's home in Coyoacán, which is filled with her art, her energy, and her stories.

The colors were rich and bright, just like her paintings. And yet, as in all of her work, there was so much pain. As a young girl, she had suffered from Polio, and a terrible bus accident left her almost paralyzed. While bedridden in a body cast, she learned to paint. Later in life, because of her ruptured uterus, she suffered numerous miscarriages. She painted her pain and sadness into her art and left a legacy of what many consider to be the greatest female painter who ever lived.

Fast forward to June of 2017, when I returned to Mexico to recover from a miscarriage and two unsuccessful attempts at IVF (in-vitro fertilization). While walking through the streets of Playa Del Carmen, I saw Frida's face everywhere. It was as if she was there to remind me. "Remember, Micaela, take your pain, like I did, and use it to create something beautiful."

I swam in the clear blue waters of Tulum and let the saltwater cleanse my sorrows. I let the magical waters wash over me to renew my strength. I ran into an old friend in Playa Del Carmen, who consoled me and listened to my story. Another angel sent by the universe, no doubt.

After a few days in Mexico, I came back to myself. Bathing in saltwater has been practiced for centuries to cure physical ailments. (1)(2) Floating in warm ocean water is my happy place. It always heals me.

I returned to California feeling rejuvenated. If Frida could turn her pain into such beautiful works of art, then I could too. I started writing this book six weeks after my return from Mexico.

The road to motherhood has been a long and winding one for me. Suffice to say that I have faith that where there is a will, there is a way. Like the ancient Mayan temples of Mexico, I persevere and thrive with time. Obstacles may come and go, but like the ocean, I move with the flow.

God's delays are not God's denials.

Reflection Questions

1. Where do you go when you feel sad or disappointed? How do you feel afterwards? Who is the person you feel safe to talk to when you feel low?

2. How could you transmute your pain or disappointment into something creative or beautiful?

3. Where is your happy place? How often do you go there?

4. Which activities make you feel stronger?

5. . Which artist do you admire? How is he or she like you?

Get Into Action

Create something beautiful. There is healing in expressing our creative self. Paint a picture, build something from wood or clay, write a story, sew a dress, compose a song, grow a garden. There are a thousand ways to be creative.

Keep your creation secret or share it with the world. It's up to you.

Remember that by sharing, we inspire each other.

Book Recommendation: Read the book *The Artist's Way* by Julia Cameron to explore your creative side. You may be surprised which talents you have hidden away which are waiting for the chance to express.

CHAPTER 30

Greece

LESSON:

Have Fun and Stay Safe

In the summer of 1989, two friends and I were riding through Europe on a Eurail Train Pass. We set sail from Brindisi, Italy for Greece.

One of my fondest memories of this trip was the boat ride over. We slept outside on the deck in our sleeping bags, watching the sunrise come up over the Adriatic Sea.

When we arrived on the docks of the island of Corfu, all the old Greek ladies dressed in black were there to greet us and offer boarding in their homes. We stayed in quaint pensiones and ate dolmades, tzatziki, and my favorite, spanakopita! YUM.

Down in Crete, we took a small boat out to a deserted island and sunbathed in the nude. Lesson number one: if you are going to sunbathe in the nude, wear sunscreen! We came back that night so sunburned, we could not sleep or sit down comfortably for several days. (And no, I won't be sharing any photos of this.)

When we got to Santorini Island, there was a lot more nightlife, and we went barhopping, just like most of the other tourists. We drank too much ouzo and laughed our butts off.

At night, we always stayed together. However, the night before we were scheduled to leave, one of my friends wanted to leave with a man she met in one of the bars. We told her to stay with us because she didn't know this man, and there were lots of drunk people. But she did not listen. She left on the back of a motorbike, and we had no idea where she went.

She was supposed to come and meet us the morning to leave for Athens. However, when she did not show up, we got very, very worried. We had no idea where she was or if she was okay. In 1989, people did not have cell phones.

We waited and waited. When the boat was about to depart, at the very last minute, she showed up totally easy-breezy. We were so mad! We said, "Why didn't you tell us where you were going?"

She replied flippantly, "Hey, I'm fine. What's the big deal?"

But it was a big deal. In all the countries I visited, I have never had an experience with violence or sexual assault. Thank goodness. However, there are cases where women disappear and get assaulted, which is why we were genuinely concerned. We were in a foreign country and did not speak the language, and to make matters worse, our friend was not sober when she left.

I have found that when it comes to traveling as a woman, it is always better to err on the side of caution. Different countries have different views and standards of what is acceptable behavior for a woman and different laws on how men are allowed to treat women.

I am always alert to people who give off a negative or strange vibe. So many times, my intuition has saved me from trouble.

The lesson here is to have fun and enjoy yourself—AND make sure that you have at least one person nearby you can call on for help, if you need it.

As the saying goes, better safe than sorry.

Reflection Questions

1. Have you ever been assaulted, harassed, or violated? Were you alone when it happened? Or were there people nearby?

2. Have you ever put yourself in a vulnerable position, such as being drunk with strangers?

3. Do you feel safe in your city? Why or why not?

4. What are some ways we can teach young girls and boys how to better respect each other and protect themselves?

5. With the recent advent of the #metoo movement, where women are voicing their experiences with abuse, do you have a #metoo story to tell? If so, have you shared it? If not, what is stopping you from sharing it?

Get Into Action

Step 1: Take a class in martial arts. I studied Karate and Judo, as well as boxing. It's a good way to stay fit and feel empowered.

Step 2: For parents, teach your child how to say "NO" if someone ever touches them inappropriately. Explain to them what is appropriate or inappropriate behavior. Do not assume they learn this in school.

CHAPTER 31

New Zealand

LESSON:

Cohabitation

In 2002, my boyfriend and I spent a total of five weeks traveling from the tip of the North Island of New Zealand to the Abel Tasman hike on the South Island. New Zealand is truly a pure and unspoiled place. The countryside is idyllic, with green hills and white, wooly sheep.

New Zealand and Alaska are the two places I have been which feel very close to heaven. We drove for miles and miles and did not see any people.

The most beautiful thing I witnessed in New Zealand is that of cohabitation of the indigenous Maori people and the English settlers. I have been to many countries which were colonized at one time in their history, such as the U.S., Canada, Cuba, Australia, Uganda, Rwanda, and the Bahamas. However, in New Zealand, I found the most cultural tolerance. Maori is the second official language.

I do not want to imply here that the effects of colonization are not felt. Subjugating a people to another country's laws and rules always has an effect. However, if you have ever met a Maori tribesman or watched the All Blacks Rugby Team, you will see why the situation was a little different in New Zealand.

First, there were fewer foreign settlers who came to live in New Zealand and second, the Maori people are fierce and proud. Most people are proud of their heritage, but not all of them are as fierce as the Maori. No offense to my English friends, but take a look at a large Maori man; he could bowl over several European men in one swoop of his fist.

I did not see a lot of intermixing and intermingling within the two groups, but I did see peaceful cohabitation.

In other countries where I have lived, including the United States, different racial groups of people live together in much more tense proximity. It saddens me to say but there still is overt and covert racism growing, like a weed, in pockets all over the world. The effects of slavery and colonization go deep into the cellular memory and have effects which last for generations. One of the reasons I write is to shed light on these dark truths.

I am happy to see that in New Zealand, the indigenous tribal customs were not squashed or sublimated and still thrive today.

May we all take a cue from them to see that even if you do not like or understand your neighbor, you can still live together harmoniously.

Reflection Questions

1. How many racial groups are there in your city or country? Are they all treated equally? Do they have the same voting, educational, and economic opportunities?

2. How many friends of different ethnic groups do you personally have? Count them. Be honest. No one is going to see your list except you. If there is one group that you do not associate with, ask yourself why not

3. Was your country colonized or invaded by another country during any time in its history? If so, by which one? And for how long? This includes military occupation. Do you know the history of your country? If not, find out. Read about it. What effects do you see and feel are still present in your society based on that colonization or occupation? There could be both positive and negative effects. List them both.

4. Are you a member of an "oppressed" or disenfranchised group? Are you female, gay, black, Latino, transgender, handicapped, Asian, etc.? How does being in this group affect your daily life? Can you think of any ways you have been mistreated because of being part of this group?

5. What are some ways we can foster more communication, understanding, and peace between various ethnic groups?

Get Into Action

Step 1: Interview someone or read the biography of someone who is part of an ethnic minority. Ask them what it felt or feels like to be repressed. Visit a section of your city where a different ethnic minority lives. Go into the stores or visit a school. Find out the conditions of how that group really lives.

Step 2: Look at your family tree or get a DNA test to find out your own ethnic makeup. You might be very surprised to learn that you have some part of your DNA belonging to an ethnic group you were not aware of.

For example, I am half-Italian. However, Italy was invaded many times by peoples from Nordic and North African tribes. One of my close friends comes from a noble family in Italy, and he has Asian ancestry. How do we know? His teeth are formed in a way that is only found in Asia.

CHAPTER 32

Hong Kong

LESSON:

The World in the Palm of Your Hand

1995 was an interesting time to be in Hong Kong, right before the Chinese government took over. Many people were fleeing and moving to Canada and Australia. Hong Kong was still part of the British Commonwealth and was set to become part of China in 1997.

The hustle and bustle of Hong Kong reminded me so much of New York City but with humid, warm, westerly winds. People spoke fast, and everywhere, someone was busy selling something. My favorite memory is of crossing the harbor by boat and taking the tram up to Victoria Peak, marveling at the breathtaking view and lights of the city below. If you go to Hong Kong, definitely make the trek to see this.

What else do I remember? First, I wish I had bought more silk! The fabrics in Hong Kong were amazing, and the tailors were incredible. You could show them a photo in a magazine, choose a fabric, and they would sew you up a tailor-made outfit in minutes!

Another great memory I have in Hong Kong was meeting an old man on the street who asked to read my palm. Now, if you know me, you know how much I love things like this. Oracle cards, I Ching, runes, palmistry, astrology, numerology—you name it. I am fascinated by them all.

So, of course, I said "yes".

What struck me was the accuracy of what he said. It is now twenty years later, and so much of what he said came true. Just like the coffee reader in Turkey—remember her?

I sat down with him on the street corner. He turned my palm over and looked at it intensely. Then he let out a loud yelp and exclaimed, "Look at all these children lines! You will have many, many children around you!" Then his face became more concerned, and he advised me in a very serious tone to use birth control because he said I was very fertile.

In 1995, China was still imposing the one child rule. (1) You can understand his concern. He did not know anything about me, nor did he know what my profession was. At that time, I was teaching elementary, then high school. Ten years later, I would start building schools for children in Africa.

I have always remembered his words. I am thankful that he

planted these seeds in my head. It would serve me well in my latter years. Many Western doctors have set ideas about the time limit of female fertility. But Asian medicine has a much more open-ended view.

Many of my healthy habits come from ancient traditions. So, my lesson for you in this chapter is to look to the wise ones. There is much to be learned from the past. Chinese, Indian, and Indigenous medicine is making a comeback because Western medicine does not have all the answers.

 How is it that a stranger that I had never met could see so much about my life just by looking at my hand?

That is a question which has intrigued me for decades. I suspect that it is the same way that our DNA codes can be garnered from our hair, skin, or saliva. One cell has imprinted inside of it a map of our whole entire body.

Aren't you curious about what your palm says about you?

Reflection Questions

1. Have you ever had your palm read? If so, how accurate was the reading? Do you think that it is a case of self-fulfilling prophecy, or that you might, in fact, have a destiny to fulfill in this lifetime?

2. Have you ever heard of the Akashic Records? It is like a life-map you create before you are born. If you could read a map of your life, what would you want to know? Where do you think you have followed your life-plan, and where do you think you have taken a detour?

3. What do you know about ancient Chinese, Indian, or indigenous medicine? Have you ever tried acupuncture, acupressure, Tai chi, shamanic healing, Aryuveda, a sweat lodge, or a Mayan massage? I will add a list of the ones I have used in the index. What has your experience been? Positive or negative? Which one are you curious to try?

Get Into Action

Choose one type of oracle reading or ancient medicine to try this week. For example, get a Mayan Massage, try Acupuncture, or have your palm read. Write down what you learned from the experience.

SIDE-NOTE

I cannot guarantee that all practitioners are as well-versed as the ones I've used. Trust your gut. Look into their eyes. Do they feel authentic to you? I have had some amazing readings, and I have also encountered some "healers" who had terrible energy. Look at how they sit with you and how they speak. Are they calm and grounded, or are they fidgety and don't look you in the eye?

For example, I recently paid a pretty penny to have a half-hour session with a woman who is quite famous. I had met her face-to-face, shook her hand, and had a ten-minute conversation with her a few days before. When I got to the session, she did not remember me at all. Makes you wonder, if she cannot remember something from a few days before, how clear is her mind? Needless to say, I will not be going back to see her ever again.

CHAPTER 33

USA

LESSON:

Cut the Cords

In 2015, my beloved father made his transition. He was my best friend, and I took care of him up to his final hours. As he left his body, I whispered into his ear, "Go toward the light, Papi." And then he was gone.

I saw his soul leave his body. I have had the gift of "sight" for all my life. I just did not always understand it. I always know when someone close to me is departing. Some might find this gift rather morbid, but I do not. It gives me much more peace about what it means to go to the other side.

After his funeral, I got into the car and drove to Sedona, Arizona, a place in the USA with very healing energy. Sedona is a small town in the middle of the most beautiful red rock canyon filled with special energy vortexes.

What is an energy vortex? It is believed that the core energy of the center of the earth is released in four places in Sedona. (1) My favorite vortex is the overview near the airport, where you can see all of the valley below. My second favorite, one which is much less frequented, is the river at the base of Cathedral Rock. It is a feminine energy vortex. Go there and immerse yourself in the water when you need to rest, heal, or call forth the Divine feminine energy.

While in Sedona, I did this special ceremony to release my father and elevate him to higher realms. I wanted his soul to be free. As a certified hypnotherapist, I learned and practiced what is called "cord-cutting". Each person we interact with closely has energetic cords which connect to us. (2) This is why break-ups and deaths are so physically and emotionally traumatic. It is not just a loss of a person. It is the loss of that energetic connection.

While most people, consciously or unconsciously, feel this connection, they do not understand why it is very important to cut the cord when the relationship is complete. I was surprised to learn in my studies that not only do we have energetic connections to people, but we also have cords which connect to specific parts of our body, or Chakras. Since our parents play such an integral role in our lives, both positively or negatively, it is helpful to recognize which parts of our bodies are energetically connected to each parent.

Let me explain in more detail. The energetic cord which I had to my father was through my third Chakra. That is around the stomach or gut area. It is our center for personal power. My father was a very powerful and charismatic individual. While growing up, I had come to depend on him to be my rock. He gave me confidence.

However, upon his passing, I needed to replace that energy. I had to garner my own confidence from within, lest my sense of self become too depleted. So, I did a ceremony to cut that cord with my father and replace the energy source from within me. Sound strange? Okay, maybe it is. But my personality has changed enormously since then. My confidence increased dramatically. People-pleasing became a thing of the past.

As a woman, I was always expected to be nice and say "yes". But powerful men, especially ones who run their own companies, are very comfortable with saying a resounding "NO" to anything that does not work for them. I started saying "NO" to a lot of things and people. Not everyone likes the new me, but I most certainly do.

Reflection Questions

1. Think carefully about each member of your close family. Which part of your body do you feel is connected to each one of them? For example, if there is someone in your family who often speaks for you or over you, most likely, he/she is connected to your throat chakra. Ask yourself if this connection is helping your or hurting you. What would happen if you were to take back your power from this person and restore that energy to yourself? How would you act differently?

2. Has anyone close to you passed away? Did/do you feel a physical loss? Think back and try to remember what exactly you missed the most. What trait or characteristic was it? Did you change after they died? Did you become more or less empowered? Why? Are you willing to try a cord-cutting ceremony to release them?

Get Into Action

Choose one person in your life that you feel you are giving away your power to. It can be a family member, boss, friend, or bully at work or school. Take your right hand and actively decide to cut through any imaginary or real energetic cords connecting you to this person. You do not have to be a certified healer to do this.

You must set a clear intention to cut the cord with that person. It does not mean you do not love the person. Nor does it mean you won't see that person anymore. It only means that you are choosing to stop giving away your power to them.

Write down who the person is and what the power is that you have been giving away. This could be your voice, your confidence, or your creativity. Sit in a quiet space. Close your eyes and imagine that person in front of you. See the cord connecting you. Take note of where the cord is connected. With your right hand, in a slow, steady movement, chop the cord away. Say a prayer and bless that person for teaching you.

Now, before you conclude, it is very important that you reconnect that energy cord back to yourself. Do not let it just dangle in the ether. Take hold of it in your mind's eye and reconnect it to yourself in the area where your power was diminished, be it your eyes, heart, gut, throat, etc. Say out loud, "I now restore myself to FULL power." Breathe deeply three times. Open your eyes.

You can do this exercise with as many people as you wish and as often as you wish. Anytime you feel weakened by another person, you are giving power away to them. Take it back.

SIDE-NOTE

This exercise does not harm or hurt anyone. It is an energetic exercise. The person you cut cords with can be alive or passed on. Cutting the cord does not take away the love you have for them or they have for you. It simply restores your power.

CHAPTER 34

England

LESSON:

Follow the Magic

When I was on that trip to Sedona, Arizona mentioned in the previous chapter, I stopped into a beautiful crystal shop called Stone Age. When I walked into the shop, I was immediately mesmerized by a huge statue of the Lady of the Lake, the mythical goddess who gave King Arthur his famous sword, Excalibur, in the legends of Camelot. For those of you who are not familiar with this history, King Arthur is considered one of the greatest kings in the history of England.

The shop owner and I had a wonderful conversation about Merlin, the famous wizard in Camelot, sacred geometry, and the island of Avalon where the Lady of the Lake was said to dwell. While there in the shop, I purchased a small pendant of the vesica pisces, which, in sacred geometry, is considered the womb of the universe. I wear that pendant to remind me to stay in my feminine power. This particular pendant was made in Glastonbury, England.

Two years later, I felt called to go this magical place that I had read about for decades. In 2017, I went on a spiritual pilgrimage to the holy city of Glastonbury, England. It is the site of the Chalice Well, Glastonbury Tor, and the famous Glastonbury Abbey, where King Arthur was buried.

What did I learn in Glastonbury? So many things, but most importantly, that magic is real and palpable.

The first item on my list was to visit Glastonbury Abbey. Then, I had a wonderful healing session with a Celtic shaman named Jeremy L. White.

He asked me to do a specific ritual at the Chalice Well. After our session together, I headed down to the Chalice Well with the magical red waters. After drinking the holy water, I said a special prayer and left a gift at the base of the Mother Mary statue as a token of my gratitude.

It was getting late in the day, and as I climbed the long steep steps up to the Glastonbury Tor, the rain was falling heavily. The temperature was below zero, and the wind was like ice. As I climbed the slippery steps, I was the only one up there high above the small town—well, me and the sheep. The wind was blowing so hard, I had to really lean in to ascend. The rain was coming down so hard, I could barely see.

The Glastonbury Tor, a large stone structure similar to those at Stonehenge, is famous for many reasons. At the exact point where the Tor stands is the intersection of two powerful lay lines: the lines of Archangel Michael and Mary, mother of Jesus. Mystics believe it is also the throat chakra center of the world. (1) I am a miracle-catcher, so I was absolutely determined to get to the top of that Tor!

Lo and behold, just as I reached the last steps, the rain stopped, the sky cleared, and the most magnificent rainbow adorned the sky right over the Tor. I was so amazed, I looked up and shouted, "Thank you, Universe!" I got a great picture of it. (See photo section.)

Legend says that both Jesus and Mary Magdalene came to Glastonbury at some point in history. Jesus' uncle Joseph lived there for many years. The famous chalice of the well was known as the Holy Grail. For thousands of years, warriors, kings, and priests searched for the elusive Holy Grail. In Glastonbury, they say that if you see a full rainbow over the Tor, you have glimpsed the Holy Grail. (2)

I will say, from standing there on the top of that hill—once the magical Island of Avalon—and gazing at one of the most beautiful things I have ever seen, that perhaps the Holy Grail is not really a cup at all. Maybe, just maybe, it is an energy, a way of being. A receptivity which, like a cup, is open and available to miracles. On that day, I truly understood what it means to be receptive to miracles.

Climb the hill. Brave the storm. Keep going. The pot of gold really does exist on the other side of the rainbow.

Reflection Questions

1. How much do you know about ancient legends of magic, such as Merlin, King Arthur, and the island of Avalon? Why do you think that TV shows and movies, such as Game of Thrones and Merlin, are so popular? Why is it that people are so fascinated by or afraid of magic?

2. Have you ever visited a holy or mystical site such as Mecca, Jerusalem, Lourdes, The Ganges, Santiago, Machu Picchu, Glastonbury, or Sedona? Did you feel anything special or different happen to you? If so, what? If you have never been, which one would you like to visit and why?

3. Have you ever made a wish or said a prayer in a special place? This includes, for example, throwing coins into a fountain or wishing on a shooting star. Do you still believe that there is magic in the world? Have your wishes come true? If you are cynical, what caused you to be this way?

Get Into Action

Create an altar. Altars do not have to be religious; they are simply a place we designate to set a specific intention or prayer. Some people make money altars, love altars, or family altars. In China, they even make kitchen altars. Choose a quiet or special place, such as your garden or a specific room in your house. Designate that place as your "sacred space". In that space, put beautiful items such as fresh flowers, crystals, candles, and photos of people you love or of things you wish to draw into your life. Put a living plant there and maybe some art. Some people put fresh fruit or chocolate. It's up to you.

You can also create a special box, called a God Box. Write down your wishes, prayers, and troubles and put them in the box. This frees up to your mind to be at peace. Having an altar in your home or garden is a way to connect with the divine daily. Each day, add a note to your God Box or something new to your altar. I like to clean and clear it every month or so and add new things.

Book Recommendation: *The Alchemist* or *The Pilgrimage* by Paolo Coehlo. Both are stories of magical journeys to mystical places which inspired me to take this trip.

CHAPTER 35

Dubai

LESSON:

Appreciation

In January 2010, I was flying back home from Uganda and had a stopover in Dubai. This is not a plug for Emirates Airlines, just an acknowledgement of a brilliant marking strategy. When I flew from Uganda, the lowest fare just happened to be with Emirates Airlines.

As you can imagine, I have flown on many different airlines in the last fifty years, and some have better service than others. I had heard very good things about Emirate Air, so I bought my ticket. At that time, all the Emirates flights leaving Uganda had an overnight stopover in Dubai, with the hotel stay included. That's what I call brilliant marketing. What a perfect way to get people to visit your country—by making a mandatory stopover and footing the bill for the hotel.

In the first chapter, I talked about my life-changing trip to Africa. After being there for almost a month, there were some things I missed from home. One of them was indoor plumbing, and the other was electricity. These are things that most of us take for granted. We assume that the tap water is going to be clean and hot and that we can plug in our cell phones and charge them anywhere. Well, not in the African countryside.

At the school in Africa, the children use an outdoor latrine. They used to only have one latrine for two hundred students, so we built more. If you have to go to the bathroom at night, you need to put on your clothes and boots and walk quite a distance to the outhouse. An outhouse is a nice name for a hole the ground, where you squat down and do your business.

I have used several outhouses on my journeys, and let's just say I could tell some horror stories. The ones with the HUGE spiders. The ones where most of the feces did not make it into the hole but were scattered next to the hole, where you have to squat down. The times when I was wearing a skirt that dragged in the mud and excrement when I bent down. The ones you had to walk a long way to in the pouring rain and mud in the middle of the night in freezing weather.

Are you starting to get the picture? Vividly? It is important that you really, really get this! Why? Well, if you cannot appreciate the squalor of the conditions, then you cannot appreciate my absolute joy when I checked into the five-star hotel in Dubai. The first thing I did was get down on my hands and knees and kiss the porcelain tile in the beautiful, sparkling-clean, newly-remodeled bathroom.

I did not even venture out much in Dubai until the next day. I spent most of the evening languishing luxuriously in my HOT bubble bath. They say we do not appreciate what we have until it's gone. There is truth to that. It is also why many western travelers, if they are completely honest, do not do much traveling in lesser developed countries. We have become, in a word, spoiled.

However, I highly recommend it to all of you. Go to a place without electricity. Give up your cell phones and laptops. Go to a place where there is no indoor plumbing. Go to a place where the women and children carry water for miles from the river just to drink. Go to a place where the water quality is so sketchy that you have to use those water purifying tablets. GO!

For if you do, you will come home a new and improved version of yourself. You will be so freaking grateful for your toilet, your bathtub, your indoor heating, your water supply, and the roof over your head. Gratitude is the energy that creates miracles. And in a world where everything comes so easily, gratitude is what seems to be in short supply.

This also works with people. That saying "absence makes the heart go fonder" is founded on this very principle. Are you an over-worked, stressed-out mom? Take a vacation without your kids or husband for a week. See how they act when you get home! Are you underappreciated at work by a demanding boss? Call in sick for a few days, and see how your boss treats you when you come back. Boyfriend ignoring you? Go on a trip with your girlfriends, and see how attentive your beau is when you return.

Sometimes, I travel to other places just to remember what an extraordinarily privileged life I have. Many of us have no idea just how good we have it.

If you have a college education, a place to live, a job, good health, some money in the bank, food on the table, clean water, indoor plumbing, and electricity, you are in the top ten percent of privilege on the planet.

There is a new phrase going around lately called "first world problems". It is when people who have everything obsess or complain about how hard their life is. I laugh when I hear this phrase because it is very apropos.

Want to put your problems into perspective?

Go live in a place where people grow their own food, or a hospital ward full of sick people, or live outdoors in a tent for a week or more. Instantaneously, your daily complaints will suddenly evaporate.

Thank you, Dubai, for being my haven at the end of a long journey. I will never, ever look at a toilet the same way again.

Reflection Questions

1. Have you ever been to a lesser developed country? What were the amenities that you missed the most? How did the people in that place live differently that you do?

2. Have you ever been away for school, work, or a vacation and come home to be treated better? Why do you think it is that we sometimes need space to appreciate the ones we love?

3. Which people in your life are you currently taking for granted? Make a list. How could you appreciate those people more? What could you do or say to show your appreciation today?

4. What are some "first world problems" that you complain about which are really not problems at all? Be honest. And if you think you do not have any, ask your friends which things you complain about that are not as big of a deal as you make them into.

Get Into Action

Choose one person whom you have not been appreciating much lately, and do something nice for them today. Start with saying, "Thank you." And be specific. Tell them all the things you really appreciate about them and what they do to you make your life better or easier. Watch them light up in delight.

Take this one step further by choosing to verbally thank everyone who does anything for you in a twenty-four-hour period. Thank the bus driver, the sales clerk, the waitress, the cashier, the mailman, the neighbor, the teacher, the friend, the child, mother, father, etc.

If we all did this every day, what would happen on the planet? They say that people hunger for appreciation more than food. A little appreciation goes a long way.

CHAPTER 36

Australia

LESSON:

Cooperation

In our around-the-world tour in 2001-2002, my boyfriend and I spent a total of five weeks traveling through Australia, or Oz, as it is affectionately called. An adventure in "Oz" is a rather fitting way to describe my trip there, as I met many wonderful traveling companions and, unfortunately, a wicked witch too. Have you ever heard the expression that having a common enemy unites people? Well, on our crazy trip to the Whitsunday Islands, that was very much true.

First, let me explain more about the Whitsunday Islands, so you can get a more vivid picture in your mind. These islands, off the East coast of Australia, south of the Great Barrier Reef, are very beautiful, full of long stretches of sand dunes and clear blue waters. They are quite wild and mostly uninhabited.

Our sailing tour left from Brisbane, and once we docked on the island, we traveled by four-by-four jeep. Traveling with your partner or close friend is always interesting as it shows you a whole new side of the other person and yourself. The rougher the terrain, the more we see people's dark side come out. Now do this with six strangers, and let's just say, s***t happens.

There were eight people in our camping group: an English couple, two Danish couples, and my boyfriend and I, from the U.S. We had two Jeeps.

What surprised me most was the chauvinism, which became apparent right from the get-go. Who was going to drive the four-by-four Jeep? Not everyone drives in Europe, and especially not large vehicles. Plus, driving a four-by-four in the sand, using a manual transmission, takes skill. At first, the men volunteered to drive. I get it—it is a masculine thing to do. Be the Alpha. Be the first driver.

However, it became excruciatingly clear straight off that the first man who volunteered did not have any experience driving a stick shift. He was grinding the gears, and we got stuck in the sand several times. Seeing how difficult it was, no one wanted to volunteer.

Now I did not want to step on anyone's toes or toot my own horn, but I am an excellent driver. I have driven through the crowded streets of Italy and grew up driving on Los Angeles freeways. So, I volunteered to drive.

That met with some macho resistance, until I got behind the wheel and was having a blast. So, lesson number one here is: when you have an important task to complete, choose the person who has the most skill, not the person who follows a gender stereotype.

Next, there was the set-up of the campsite. This takes a team effort. The tents were large and unwieldy, and we had to make a fire to cook our own food. There were wild dingoes (wild dogs) on the island, which have been known to snatch and eat small children, so we had to make our camp close to each other and close to the fire. It was a little like watching that program Survivor. Boy, did we wish we could have voted someone off our team on that trip, but I am getting ahead of myself.

I don't remember now how many days we camped, but it felt like an eternity. Over the course of a few hours, it became abundantly clear that one person—a woman—was not interested in doing any activity which would wreck her precious manicure. And she, the wicked witch, became our common enemy. The more she complained about the dirt, the sand, the cold, the food, the bugs, the more we rolled our eyes. She frequently spoke disdainfully about us in her native language to her boyfriend. However, there were people in the group who could understand her, and they became more and more incensed and embarrassed by her lack of diplomacy or cooperation.

At the time of this trip, I was thirty-four years old. If I went on the same trip now, I would handle it very differently. I did not understand then just how much one's energy and thoughts can affect a group, both positively or negatively. This woman became our nemesis. Everyone except her boyfriend began to despise her. And the more we despised her, the worse she got.

During the trip, I suffered horribly because of the insect bites I got all over my body and especially on my feet. I cried at night because the itching was killing me and scratched my feet until they bled. As you can imagine, my patience and tolerance were at an all-time low.

Since this book is about lessons, let me explain what I learned in hindsight. One of my favorite books is called You Can Heal Your Life by Louise Hay, mentioned in Chapter 12. I read it for the first time a few years after this trip. If I had read it before, this trip would have played out very differently. In this book, Louise, through her years of being a spiritual counselor, amassed an encyclopedia of information on the energetic causes for disease in the body. If you look up insect bites, you will see that the energetic cause is that we are letting someone else get under our skin, literally. (1)

The more irritated I became with this woman, the more I scratched. And since I was scratching so much, my body started to have an auto-immune reaction. By the time I got back to Brisbane a few days later, the pharmacist took one look at me, covered in over two hundred and fifty red bumps, and gave me such a strong antihistamine that I slept for three days straight. No exaggeration.

Do you think I was letting that woman get under my skin? You do the math.

I screamed at my boyfriend at one point on the trip that I wanted to strangle her. Not very enlightened of me, I know, but I was extremely sleep-deprived and in a terrible amount of discomfort. Want to really know your partner? Watch how they act when they are very sick. Hello, dark side!

The irony is that it was my energy that was making my condition worse.

There are many ways to handle difficult people, and I highly recommend that you choose a way that does not involve making yourself sick! The more I despised her, the worse I got. And that energy just kept causing things to get worse on the trip. It was like a comedy of errors—flat tires, rain storms, jellyfish, bed bugs on the boat, cuts, bruises, scrapes. And now I know that it was not her who was the cause of the problem. It was my (our) reaction to her.

So, the next time you have someone around you who irritates you, ask yourself, "Is this really worth me getting upset over?" If you knew beyond a shadow of a doubt that your dislike or irritation would turn back upon you, would you react differently? That's the rub. There is no way to avoid it. Even when we think that we might have gotten away with doing something unkind or unlawful, that energy always comes back to us. That's why they say Karma is a b***h.

Reflection Questions

1. Who in your life is irritating you? How are you responding to them? On a scale of 1-10, how much are they bothering you? If the number is higher than a 5, consider all the ways that your irritation is swirling back to you causing you more harm. Can you find a new way of dealing with that person?

2. Have you ever been on a team where one person does very little to contribute? How does this make you feel? Are you the one who does more or less in a group?

3. Think of a time you went on a trip or lived with someone when they or you were sick. How did their/your behavior change? What did you learn about yourself or your partner when you went through a difficult time together? Did it bring you closer or tear you apart?

4. Think about a time you viewed someone as an enemy or rival. Did this person spur you to become a better or worse version of yourself? Why?

Get Into Action

Go on a group tour. Cooperation is a skill that is learned and practiced. Ask anyone parenting a two-year-old, and they will tell you that cooperation is not necessarily an innate trait. Finding ways to practice cooperation is especially useful for those who have no siblings or live alone. It is so easy to get set in our ways if we do not use the cooperation muscle.

CHAPTER 37

Laos

LESSON:

Innocence

In late 2001, my boyfriend and I had been traveling in Southeast Asia for several months. By the time we got to Laos, it was like a breath of fresh air.

Laos is a small country nestled between Vietnam and Thailand. Many people have never heard of it or been there. At the time we went, not many Western tourists had arrived, and we were greeted with warmth and curiosity. My favorite memories of Laos were of Luang Prabang, with its golden doors, silk fabrics, and French colonial architecture. Most of the villages were farm villages, so we woke up each morning to the chorus of all the local roosters competing for top billing.

I will never forget the children who followed me down the street, laughing and smiling, because they had never seen someone who looked like me. A bus full of children passed by, and all the children smiled and waved at us. There was an air of innocence in Laos that I had not ever encountered before.

This is not to say that Laos was not affected by the wars and destruction in Vietnam and Cambodia. But there was a different energy in Laos. It was as if the people had somehow kept their joy. It is hard for me to put into words, but it was a tangible feeling.

People think of borders as places where you stop, and they stamp your passport. However, I think and feel that they are much more than that. They are energetic boundaries. Have you ever been in Italy and crossed into Switzerland? There is a palpable change in energy, even at a distance of twenty kilometers (ten miles). The people think, act, talk, and dress differently.

In Laos, the people walk and speak slower than their neighbors. Everything in Laos is more laid-back.

In fact, I found Laos to be so peaceful that when my visa expired, I crossed into Thailand, stamped my passport, and went back to Laos for several more weeks. It was as if my body just needed to be somewhere to rest.

Laos is like a Southeast Asian oasis. There are rivers to float down and guest houses to relax in. We had been backpacking for about six months at this point, and we needed a vacation from our vacation. Trying to see too much in too short a time is exhausting. Changing time zones, languages, environments, and diets is a mental and physical shock.

My advice: take your time when you travel. I have encountered many sick travelers over the years, some even deathly ill with malaria or dysentery. I myself have had a few unpleasant bouts in foreign hospitals, even an emergency appendectomy in a hospital where I did not understand the doctors or nurses. It was painful, scary, and lonely.

Obey the body if it needs to rest. Go to a place where life is peaceful.

Hakuna Matata. (1)

Reflection Questions

1. Think about a nearby town, state, or county not so far but that has a very different pace or language or lifestyle. How do the people live or act differently than you do? Are they faster or slower? How do you feel when you go to that place?

2. What kind of vacations do you usually take? Relaxing ones or adventure treks? Do you plan family road trips like in the movie Vacation with Chevy Chase? How did you feel after your last vacation? Rested or exhausted?

3. In one of my favorite books called The Tao of Pooh, the author writes about the "busybacksons". These are the people who are always in a rush, full of things to do. Even when they lie down, their mind is buzzing full of details. Are you a busybackson? Do you find it difficult to go to sleep? What are some ways you could change your habits to be more restful?

Get Into Action

Getting adequate sleep and rest is vital to your health. Practice these habits before bedtime.

- Drink no caffeine after five p.m.

- Turn off the news and do not watch violent movies or play video games before bed.

- Take all electronic devices out of your bedroom while you sleep.

- Turn off the wi-fi signal at night and turn your cell phone off or put it on airplane mode.

- Do not eat a heavy dinner full of carbs and/or red meat. Keep your dinner at light as possible.

- Do some light stretching exercises before bed.

- Set the intention that when you wake up the next morning, you will rise feeling rested and energized.

Book Recommendation: The Tao of Pooh by Benjamin Hoff, which is a beautiful little tale of ways to lead a simpler, stress-free life.

CHAPTER 38

USA: *Hawaii*

LESSON:

The Light and Dark Sides of Ourselves

In September of 2017, my husband and I got married on Kukio Beach, on the beautiful island of Hawaii.

Hawaii has such a sacred place my heart, I have given it its own chapter. Up until 1898, it was an independent country and still maintains its royal family line. I have been to Hawaii five times in my life. Each time I went, it was a very transformational experience. The Hawaiian legends have their own gods and goddesses, and many people believe Hawaii to have a strong healing energy. This energy is called Mana. The Hawaiians pay homage to the gods and revere many holy sites, such as the

Birthing Stones, where queens gave birth to kings. (1)(2)

We had our wedding on a private beach, which is designated as protected land because of its links to the ancient Hawaiian culture. For our wedding, we spent the first week on the sunny side of the island, which is the Kona side. Everything was light and happy and exciting. We were full of hope and had the most romantic and beautiful ceremony I could have ever imagined. We did it Hawaiian-style, with salute of the conch shell, the Lei (flower) blessing, and the calling in of the ancestors to bless us and guide us. After imagining my wedding for so many years, it was just like I envisioned it to be.

The second week, we drove over to the other side of the island, known as the rainy side. It is where Volcano National Park is, and the sand is black from the molten lava. While there, we stayed at a special place called the Magic Lava Temple. It is a unique accommodation built right on the Kapalana Lava Flow, at the base of the Kilauea volcano.

We had been studying sound healing and wanted to experience a crystal sound bath on the lava.

Before we started the sound bath, we said a prayer and blessing to the goddess Pele, who is the Goddess of Fire. There are many tales of her in Hawaii, as she is the goddess who created the lava, which, in turn, created the Hawaiian Islands. Pele is known as a creator and destroyer, for lava creates new land, but it also destroys everything in its path.

As a healer, I have done many kinds of healing in many sacred places. But I was not prepared for the magnitude of the change which occurred following our sound bath. It was as if, like the black sand, we were plunged into our own inner darkness. We went from happy newlyweds to bickering rivals.

It was a shock to the system. Pele is considered the Goddess of Transformation, so asking for her help requires that one pull up all the internal blocks in the way of achieving that wish. Each day that went by after that ceremony, our demons came forth, stronger than ever.

At one point, while I was swimming in the water, surrounded by the sea turtles, I cut my right toe on the sharp lava rock. I didn't feel it at first, but I looked down and the ocean had turned red. Blood swirled all around me. I was overjoyed to swim with the turtles, but once I realized how profusely I was bleeding, I limped out of the water, calling for help. My husband was on the other side of the beach and could not hear me.

Finally, I got to the lifeguard station, and they bandaged me up. I knew intuitively, since we were so close to the volcano, that this was a message from Pele. I asked several Hawaiians what they thought about what happened. They all said the same thing: "Pele demands a sacrifice."

"What does that mean?" I asked. They told me that in the legend, Pele demands a sacrifice of blood, urine, or semen. I had asked her to help us create a baby. The sacrifice she demanded was my blood.

I meditated on it for several weeks after I got home. What did the blood have to do with my request? One day, the answer came to me. Just as I have mentioned in previous chapters, if you want to interpret the signs from the other side, you need to pay attention. I was swimming with turtles when I got cut. Those turtles I had been searching for years. They always seemed to elude me. And yet, on that day, on that beach, they were everywhere. The turtles were so close to me, I could touch them. And not only that—they were laying their eggs.

I believe in animal messengers, and it was no coincidence that I finally found the turtles that day. Pele was showing me the answer to my question. "If you want eggs, you must bleed. You have to act like a turtle."

To translate that, I am fifty years old. Most women at fifty no longer menstruate. As women age, their bodies produce less estrogen and progesterone, so there is no need for a monthly menses because they are not ovulating. I won't get too technical here, but for me to have a good, strong pregnancy, I needed to be producing fresh, healthy blood.

Pele was showing me how to do that. "Slow down," she said. "Be like a turtle."

In the West, women suffer from all kinds of maladies because their bodies are overworked, overstressed, and overtired. As a holistic practitioner, I saw so many cases of early onset menopause, thyroid problems, infertility, and a host of other problems because women were not getting enough down-time. Pregnancy at any age needs rest. Pregnancy at fifty demands rest.

So, there it is. Pele spoke to me, and I have listened. Once we left the island, there were still remnants of the dark energy emerging to be healed, and it took three months for us to complete the healing process.

Was it what I expected from the first three months of marriage? No.

However, was it necessary? For us, yes. Once we emerged from the darkness, our relationship was stronger than ever.

I have heard so many stories of people going to Hawaii to heal.

Some people stay for a short time. Some stay for years. I know I will go back. Another legend about Pele is that if you bleed on her island, she is inviting you back.

I see the island of Hawaii as a metaphor for marriage. There is a light side and a dark side. Together, they create a whole.

The divorce rate is high in my state of California, upwards of fifty percent. Having witnessed many weddings and divorces of friends, I have a theory as to one reason why the divorce rate is so high here. There is too much hype around the wedding, and not enough emphasis on the relationship. Everyone wants a big party, a fancy dress, and a diamond ring. But there is no preparation for what happens after the "happily ever after". No one tells you that marriage is a marathon, not a sprint. Couples invest thousands of dollars in the wedding, but little time investing in pre-marriage counseling. My husband and I did meet with a spiritual counselor before our wedding, and I am very glad we did.

All things which go up must come down. And unfortunately, when most couples hit the dark side, they shut down, cheat on their spouse, or run away. The darkness is not pleasant. It is downright uncomfortable. The shadow side of our subconscious will reflect all of our least favorite qualities back at us through our partner. Most people do not have the tools to cope when things get hard.

I have my spiritual tools, many of which I am sharing in this book. I share this in hopes that we will all have more compassion and understanding when faced with our own dark shadow. When we love someone, this shadow side will emerge because it feels safe to be seen. It wants to heal. We cannot heal what we cannot feel.

So, to conclude, I say this: Marriage is not for the faint of heart. As much as I desired to find my soulmate when I was younger, I simply was not ready to go through the storm. Pele, the Goddess of Transformation, is known as wrathful, but she is also the bringer of great bounty and abundance. If you can face both the light and dark sides of yourself, you will be made whole.

Once lava cools, it is one of the hardest substances known to man. It becomes solid and strong. Once you heal your shadow, you, too, will become much stronger. No one can heal it but you. You must have the courage to go through the fire to get to the other side.

Mahalo Nui Loa, Pele. Thank you for the lesson, beautiful goddess.

Reflection Questions

1. Have you ever been married? Would you like to get married? Do you feel amply prepared for the peaks and valleys of a long-term relationship? How well do you handle conflict?

2. What are the dark sides of your personality? Do you hide this side of yourself? Whom do you feel safe enough to show it to? What are some ways that this dark side has shown up to sabotage you?

3. What kind of support network do you have when things are challenging in your life? Do you have someone whom you can share your true feelings with? Can you share with your family? And if not, why?

4. If you are single, what are some ways you could practice commitment in your life right now? For example, could you commit to a mortgage, an organization, a coaching program? If you are in a relationship, what are some ways you could deepen your commitment to your partner? If you have misgivings about getting married, what are they? Have you discussed them with your partner? If no, why not? Are you willing to see a pre-wedding counselor?

Get Into Action

Commit to one thing in your life that is challenging for you for at least thirty days, such as sticking to a fitness plan, running a marathon, doing a vegan diet, or saving a specific amount of money for something important. Notice how you respond or react when the impulse arises to quit. As T. Harv Ekert, author of Secrets of The Millionaire Mind, says, "how you do anything is how you do everything." If you quit, start again. If you fall off the wagon for a few days, recommit to starting again. Commitment is a muscle. It gets stronger with practice.

CHAPTER 39

Monaco

LESSON:

Act As If

The year was 1992. I was in France for the summer, studying French. Some of my classmates and I decided to take a day trip to Monaco.

Now, if you know the story of Princess Grace (Grace Kelly), you know that Monaco is one of the wealthiest and most glamorous places on the planet. The Casino of Monte Carlo is legendary, made famous by many a James Bond film. (1) Glitterati, royalty, sheiks, and barons all congregate there to play and mingle with the rich and the famous.

I remember walking through the casino in Monaco and thinking that it was just like in the movies—stylish people dressed to the nines, Ferraris, diamonds, champagne, etc. We had a fabulous time that night, and I learned a valuable lesson that has served me well.

There is great truth in the saying that "you become like the people you spend most of your time with". The rich get richer not by accident. The rich get richer because they have great business connections and a wealthy mindset. Billionaire Sir Richard Branson says that billionaires think with a billionaire mindset. If you have a poverty consciousness, you will always remain broke. It is a universal law of energy.

I am not saying that being rich makes you a better human. It only makes you more of who you already are. If you are kind and generous, you simply become more generous. If you are petty and insecure, you become an arrogant jerk.

In one of my favorite books, The Success Principles by Jack Canfield mentioned in Chapter 1, he writes about "The Poker Chip Theory of Success". It goes like this: the more success you have experienced in your life, the more willing you will be to take risks. It is like betting in poker. If you have a lot of chips to bet, you will bet more. If you only have one measly chip, you will probably hold on to that chip for dear life. How do you get more chips? You take more risks.

I always recommend taking things in baby steps. Start with setting a small goal. The first time I went abroad alone, I went for one month on a foreign exchange program. It gave me taste of what it would feel like being abroad. After completing my month successfully, I was willing to go again—this time, for a year. I saw many of my students get disappointed because they would take on a challenge that was too big, then give up midway and feel like a failure.

Remember that the more success you have, no matter how small, builds up your confidence.

If you ever get the chance to go to Monte Carlo, go to the casino. Watch the players betting at the high-stakes tables. Watch their body language, so cool under pressure. Those folks have been playing the game of life for years. You do not get good at anything without practice.

And pay attention to whom you spend the most time with. If you want to be rich, you need to learn to think and act like a wealthy person does.

They did many studies in the U.S. on lottery winners. Most winners, one year after winning thousands or even millions of dollars, go back to the same "money set point" they were at before winning. (2) In other words, the poor people had spent all the money and were broke (3), and the wealthy people had invested the money to make it grow. Ironically, the same is also true for their levels of happiness. Having more money did not make the winners happier. (4)

Our habits make or break us. Walk around Rodeo Drive in Beverly Hills, or another very wealthy neighborhood, and watch the people. Look at how they dress, walk, and talk. If you want something, you need to draw it to you by believing that you deserve to have it and that it is coming to you.

Unfortunately, most people have the equation backwards. They think their lives will change once they get the thing they want. Energy does not work like that. If you act and think like you are already there, you will magnetize it much faster.

When I worked part-time while attending photography school at night, my monthly income was only fifteen hundred U.S.

dollars per month, which, in the U.S., is just above the poverty line. I went on trips, had nice clothes, and drove a nice car, not on credit. I did not get any loans at that time. I never thought or felt like a poor person, so I never acted like one.

If you want to rise above your current circumstance, you need to start surrounding yourself with people who are more successful that you are.

My final advice here is very important. I used to say this repeatedly when I taught in the business program at university. Do not take advice on money from someone who does not have any. Likewise, do not ask for dating advice from someone who does not have the kind of relationship you want.

Why? Because if someone does not have it, they do not know how to create it.

Seems obvious, right? But unfortunately, every day, people ask for advice from the wrong people and get more of what they don't want.

Want to learn how to invest money? Read an article by Warren Buffet. Don't ask your cousin Vinny, who lives in a run-down apartment.

I hope I have made my point.

Reflection Questions

1. What is something that you would like to manifest more of? Money, sex, love, vacation? Why do you want this thing? Do you think that having it would make your life better? Why or why not?

2. What are your current money habits? Do you save? Invest? Own or rent property? How much do you owe in debt? Do you donate any money to charity? Who in your family has good money habits? If no one in your family does, who else do you know that has good money habits?

3. If you had a poker chip for every success you have ever had, how many poker chips would you have? (Even small successes count.) Make a list.

4. What is one area of your life you do not take risks in? Why not?

5. Choose someone famous you admire. Find out more about this person. Read their biography, if available. What habits led to their success? How could you start emulating this person today?

Get Into Action

Choose something you want, such as a job at a specific company. Go to that company or nearby, where you can observe the people who work there. How do they dress? Talk? Walk? Ask around and see if anyone you know has any contacts at that company. Ask questions. See if you could interview that person. Each company has corporate culture, and you need to discover if it is a good fit for you.

If you want to get married, for example, go to a bridal store. Try on the dresses and see how they feel. I did this one year before I met my husband.

Choose something that you can act as if you already have it and get moving. Take action. Each step you take moves you closer to your goal.

Book Recommendations: Read T.Harv Eker's *Secrets of The Millionaire Mind* or Anthony Robbins' *Awaken The Giant Within* to change your mindset around money.

CHAPTER 40

Ethiopia

LESSON:

Past Lives

In 2010, my flight to Uganda landed in Addis Ababa, Ethiopia to take on more passengers. I only stayed in Ethiopia for approximately one hour, so, you might be wondering why I would include a chapter on it.

Well, I want to talk a little bit about a topic that may surprise many of you: past lives. If you are absolutely opposed to this idea, skip over this chapter. If you are even a little bit curious, keep reading.

If you are a Buddhist or a Hindu, you already believe in reincarnation, so this will seem very normal to you. If you are not sure where you stand on reincarnation, read on.

I am not Buddhist or Hindu, although I have studied both religions. I am an equal opportunity believer, which means that I believe that God is non-denominational. I respect the right of each person to believe in whatever god they choose.

This book is not about religion, nor am I trying to convince anyone what to believe. It is simply a compilation of my own experiences and what I have learned from them.

Back to Ethiopia...

Have you ever felt deeply called to go to a certain place, although you don't know why? Have you ever met someone and had the feeling of deja vu?

Well, for most of my life, I felt called to go to Africa. In fact, I almost went several times. But something always got in the way. When I finally did go, I had such a feeling of déjà vu. I used to think that if I went to Africa, I might not ever want to come home. And as you know from my chapter on Uganda, I did leave part of my heart in Africa and am forever connected to it in a deep and profound way.

I have always been curious about the topic of reincarnation and past lives. For as long as I can remember, I've read everything I could get my hands on regarding this topic.

In 2011, when I became a certified hypnotherapist, I specifically studied the branch of hypnosis called Past Life Regression. (1) As a student and later a practitioner, I have experienced several past life regression sessions.

When I landed in Ethiopia in 2010, I did not know why I had such a feeling of recognition, only that I felt like I had been there before. It started coming back as I walked through the streets in Africa, surrounded by men who escorted me from place to place. I had the distinct feeling of having lived that experience already. It was the strangest sensation. I felt memories coming back of having been protected and guarded at one point in time.

During several past life regression sessions I did in 2011 and 2015,

I experienced clear and vivid memories of being a member of the royal family in the Kingdom of Nubia. The Kingdom of Nubia, according to historians, existed from 2500 BC to the 4th Century AD, in what is now the region of Sudan and Southern Egypt, very close to Addis Ababa, Ethiopia. (2) In my memories, I saw that I lived in a castle and was protected by many bodyguards. So what does any of this have to do with now?

Well, it changed my sense of worthiness. In my past life, I was protected and guarded because I was a person of high stature. I have researched the time period, and there was a figure in history who closely matches the memories that came back to me. All I can say for certain is that after returning from Africa, I was a changed person in so many ways.

One of the most profound ways I changed was that I felt more worthy. My African name, given to me by the family I lived with, is Mugisha. It means "gift" in their language. I felt valued and cherished in a way I had never felt before.

I do not know for certain if I did have another life in Africa sometime in the past. But I do know that I am a different person because of my trip in 2010.

One thing that many people suffer from is a sense of

unworthiness. Do I really deserve to be happy, wealthy, and deeply cherished? I saw time and time again in counseling others one-on-one that these feelings of unworthiness caused people to choose unhealthy relationships, settle for less, choose self-destructive habits, etc.

It took many years for me to truly feel worthy of being deeply loved. Our parents can only love us as much as they themselves felt loved. To feel worthy of having a wonderful life, we sometimes must break out of an unhealthy family pattern. To do something that no one in one's family has done takes a lot of courage and self-worth. If the feeling of worthiness is not present, we will cave under the first sign of criticism.

There are many ways to learn how to feel worthier. Here, in this chapter, I am posing a radical new idea: What if we really have lived past lives? What if we could access all the lessons and knowledge we learned in those lives and utilize that information now? Good or bad, each experience teaches us something.

As I have gone deeper into my study on brain research, I have found that we all have DNA or cellular memory, mentioned in previous chapters. Memories from ancestors and even past lives are stored in the vast web of neurons in our brain and bodies.

What would we be capable of if we could access this data?

I know for sure that after coming home from Africa, I was a changed woman. Something there felt like HOME to me in way that I never felt while living in other places.

I challenge you, the reader, to follow up on your intuition. Which place is calling you? Go. See what happens.

Reflection Questions

1. Write down a time when you felt a strong sense of déjà vu. Where were you? Who were you with? What exactly made you feel like you had been there before?

2. Have you heard of hypnosis? Have you ever tried it? Would you be willing to try it? Why or why not?

3. Do you believe in reincarnation? Why or why not?

4. What do you think would be possible if we could access our ancestral memories? Would this be a positive thing or negative thing in your opinion?

5. Why did you choose your profession? Did you feel a calling? Where do you think that impulse came from? When you were a child, did you have any skills or talents that just came naturally to you, without any training?

6. Which place feels magnetic to you? Have you gone yet? If not, why not? If you went already, how did you feel once you got there? Do you feel there was an important reason you went? If so, what was that reason?

Get Into Action

In Western Astrology and Kabbalistic Astrology, there are two important point in your natal astral chart called the North Node and the South Node. The North Node, according to astrologers, is where you are going in this lifetime, and the South Node shows you how you lived in your past life.

Go to www.astro.com to get your free astral chart done. Look under the personal profile section and find your North/South Node.

The best book I have ever read on the North and South Nodes is called Astrology of the Soul by Jan Spiller. In it, you will find a detailed description of how your past life patterns affect your current life and why some patterns feel so hard to break. After considerable study and research on this subject and reading many of my clients' astral charts, I highly recommend that you read this book.

Once I learned about my North/South nodes, which happen to be in Aries and Libra, so many of my life choices and challenges made sense. Knowing where my soul intended to go in this life helped me align with my own "True North."

I will let you read the book and decide for yourself.

Step 2: If you are open to it, contact a hypnotherapist who specializes in Past Life Regression in your city and see what you discover about your own memories.

Book Recommendations: If you are interested in the topic of astrology, I also encourage you to read *Jupiter Signs* by Madlyn Aslan on how your astral chart relates to your relationship with money and *Kabbalistic Astrology* by Rav Berg to understand your astrological karma.

CHAPTER 41
China

LESSON:
Discipline

In 1994, I crossed the border into China from Hong Kong, which, at that time, was a separate country. I stayed in the province of Shenzhen.

What did I notice in China? Well, for starters, the crowds. When you hear that China has over one billion people, it does not feel real until you go and experience what this feels like in person. Not all of China is densely populated, but the area I went to, Shenzhen, has between 12 and 20 million people, just in one city! (1)

How does the size of the population affect the culture? China is a communist country. Therefore, there is much more emphasis on the collective good. One key tenet of the Communist system is: what is good for the group is more important than what is good for the individual.

Many of you may balk at this concept, especially if you are used to having a lot of freedom. I grew up in a place where I had a lot of freedom. However, having a lot of freedom comes with a price tag too. China is well known for having intense academic competition and precision athletes, both of which take immense discipline. Growing up with a Chinese stepfather, I often rebelled against having to follow strict rules and living under such high expectations.

In California, discipline is not revered—quite the opposite, in fact. Looking back at my life, however, I can see how having learned to be more disciplined in my thinking made me more successful. Discipline is needed to finish things, to reach a goal, to curb the desire for instant gratification in order to gain the long-term rewards. I am not saying that I believe that we should all turn into strict disciplinarians and have no fun at all. There needs to be a balance.

One topic that I have talked a lot about in this book is health. And being fit and healthy at fifty—or any age—requires discipline, not just in what I choose to eat but also in exercising and focusing my mind on what I want to achieve.

It is interesting to note that the original meaning of the word "discipline" comes from "disciple" or "devotee", as in the twelve disciples of Jesus. Disciplina, in Latin, means "instruction" or "knowledge", so disciples were, in essence, students. Nowadays, the word "discipline" in English has become more associated with punishment than with learning. However, being "disciplined" or completely devoted to a skill is not necessarily a bad thing. In fact, it is that kind of focus which creates mastery.

There are many things I have learned and practiced that originated in China: acupuncture, acupressure, the I Ching, the Tao, Feng Shui, T'ai Chi, and massage. There are also some ancient Chinese medicine secrets that I use daily, such as the concept of Yin (feminine) and Yang (masculine) energies. Everything in Chinese medicine is about balancing these two polarities. So many health issues prevalent today are related to an imbalance in the body, for example: thyroid problems, infertility, heart attacks, anxiety, insomnia, cancer, and obesity, to name a few.

In order to cure these diseases, the body must be in balance. (2)

I have included a list of ways to get one's body back in balance in the reference section for this chapter. (3)

The oldest living man in the last century was a Chinese herbalist and martial artist named Li Ching Yun. He lived to be 197 years old. (4) When asked what his secret longevity, this was his reply: "Keep a quiet heart, sit like a tortoise, walk sprightly like a pigeon, and sleep like a dog." (5)

I have not been to China in many years, so I do not know how many people there still use these ancient practices. I use them every day, and doing so requires discipline.

I am grateful that I have learned to balance both the Yin and the Yang. As a teacher and parent, I see how important balance is. Too much discipline creates resentments and stifles creativity. However, little or no discipline creates apathy and lack of integrity. In the reflection questions, we will look at how to create more balance in our lives.

Reflection Questions

1. Where is your life out of balance? In your health? Your finances? Your love life? How could you act in a way that is more balanced?

2. On a scale of 1-10, how disciplined are you? Do you finish what you start? Do you honor your word? Are you often late? Do you eat food that makes you feel sick and then berate yourself afterwards? Think of someone you know who has used discipline to reach a goal that you admire. What are some ways you could be more disciplined in your life?

3. As a parent, are you too much of a disciplinarian, or are you too lax? Do you provide a consistent structure for your children, or do you often change the rules or give in easily? How is this behavior affecting your child(ren)? How is it affecting you? What is an area you could be more consistent in? What is an area you would like your children or your spouse to improve in? How could you model this behavior for them?

4. Think of a goal you set that you did not complete, such as finishing school or completing a project. What stopped you? What are the benefits you gain from not finishing? Be honest. How do you feel about not finishing? What could you do differently to complete the task?

Get Into Action

Choose one thing in your diet that is not good for you, either because it is causing you to gain extra weight or because you feel tired or bloated after eating it. For thirty days, eliminate that food or drink from your diet. Start with one thing, such as candy, pizza, red meat, dairy, caffeine, alcohol, or gluten. If you miss a day, keep adding on extra days until you complete the whole thirty days.

Write in your journal how you feel once you gave it up. Do you feel better? Do you feel proud of yourself?

Once you complete the thirty days, give yourself a reward, big or small. It is important to be rewarded after reaching a goal. This reprograms our brains to enjoy a new habit.

CHAPTER 42

Guatemala

LESSON:

What To Do
in the Meantime

On the way to Costa Rica in 1997, I stopped over in Guatemala. Since it was a layover, I did not see much of the countryside. However, I have a vivid memory of seeing the most beautiful volcano coming through the mist as we landed. It was near sunrise, and it was a magnificent sight to behold.

The ancient Mayan civilization spanned through the southern part of Mexico and into Guatemala. When I return to Guatemala, the first place I will go is to the pyramids at Tikal. There is much wisdom to be learned from this ancient civilization.

What I want to share in this chapter is the importance of stopovers in our life. Many people ask me how to manifest money, relationships, optimal health, happiness, etc. While there is such thing as the Law of Attraction, I believe that manifestation, like happiness, is a journey, not a destination. The universe can and will bring us things we ask for. However, there will be stopovers along the way.

Some of you will be rolling your eyes here. "Why? Why do I have to wait?" you cry. I know, I did the same so many times myself.

Here is why there are stopovers...

We simply are not ready to receive what we have asked for. Once we are ready or in alignment with it, it does manifest.

The stopovers are here to prepare us to receive, to make us more receptive and grateful along the way.

Let me give you an example from my own life and from the statistics of California lottery winners. Back in Chapter 39, I mentioned the study they did on the lottery winners, remember? The study showed that even if people won one million dollars or more, after one year, they went right back to where they were financially and mentally before they won.

How can this be? It is because of what Abraham Hicks calls our set point. (1) We will keep creating the same result over and over to match our set point. It is bizarre but real. I have seen people with millions of dollars get sued and lose it all because their set point was low.

This same thing happened to me in relationships. I would meet a great man, everything would go well, and then eventually,

I would sabotage myself. It is like a form of emotional bankruptcy. At first, I wanted to blame the other person. "I keep meeting 'commitment-phobes'," I'd say, but the cold, hard truth is that I was drawing to me mirrors of myself. We draw to us what is similar in vibration. This is what the law of attraction means.

So, those jobs that you didn't like or those relationships which didn't quite work, they were all stopovers to bring you to the next step or the next set point.

No one says a prayer that goes like this: "Dear God (Universe), please bring me a wonderful man whom I will divorce in six months" or "Please bring me a wonderful job with a boss who hates me."

No one in their right mind asks for these things.

We ask for the job or the relationship or the child or the million dollars. What most of us do not know is that if we get those things before we are ready, we will destroy them.

When I was nineteen years old, I met the most wonderful man. We loved each other deeply for five years. But even though I said I wanted to get married, I was not ready. So, I sabotaged my own relationship. Fortunately, we are still good friends all these many years later.

My point is that even if you think you are ready, you might not be. It is a bitter pill to swallow. Trust me, I know.

However, the other option is even worse. Getting what you want and then destroying it is much more emotionally devastating. It takes a toll on not just you, but everyone around you.

So, the next time you are on the fast track to getting something or someone, and the universe gives you a stopover, look out the window, enjoy the view, and know that this stopover is a good thing. By the time you get to your destination, you will be wiser, more grateful, and more in alignment with keeping it.

Reflection Questions

1. Think about the "stopovers" in your life. Where did you stop? What did you learn from that stopover? Did you arrive at your destination? Or are you still en route?

2. What are some ways you could enjoy the journey more fully today? Are you focusing too much on not having something (money, baby, soulmate, university degree, etc.)? How is this feeling affecting the other people in your life? Are you grateful for all the good things which are already here? Who or what is something good that is already here which you could enjoy more?

3. Think of a time you got something you really wanted. How did you feel afterwards? Were you excited or deflated? Did you immediately move on to the next goal or thing? Why? On a scale of 1-10, how addicted are you to "getting things"? Does getting make you feel happier?

4. Choose one thing you really want right now. Ask yourself, "Why do I really want it? How do I think it will make me feel? Can I feel happy without it? Can I let it go for a while? Is it something I really want, or is it something I think I should have? Is someone else pressuring me to get it? Am I comparing myself to what other people have? If so, why?"

Get Into Action

1.Try going for one week without thinking or talking about something you want to manifest. Just let it go for seven days. Take a breather. Do things that make you feel happy and grateful. Write down what happens during those seven days. How do you feel after the seven days are over? Did you notice any changes? Letting go allows the space for a new possibility to occur.

2.Listen to one of Abraham-Hicks' talks on www.abraham-hicks.com or YouTube. Write down in your journal something interesting you learned.

Book Recommendation: *Ask and It is Given* by Esther and Jerry Hicks. In this book, you will find the Emotional Set Point Chart and ways to raise your vibrational frequency to attract more abundance.

CHAPTER 43

Nepal

LESSON:

Synchronicity

In 2001, while we were backpacking in Thailand, we went to the travel agency to book a flight to Nepal. I had heard many wonderful stories about adventures in Kathmandu, the capital city of Nepal. We were planning on leaving that week.

The same day we went to buy our ticket, we found out that the crown prince of Nepal had just assassinated the king, queen, and several other members of the royal family. Riots and chaos had broken out all over the country. (1) All the flights were cancelled or delayed. What a shock! We immediately changed our flight plans.

I read a book about miracles recently called *God Doesn't*

Create Miracles, You Do by Yehuda Berg. It explains that there are three kinds of miracles. One type is called an Avoidance Miracle, which is a miracle that protects us from danger. These miracles happen all the time in our lives, whether we know it or not. If we had left even one day sooner, we would have been in Nepal on the day of the assassination. Who knows what would have happened to us? There was rioting and looting, and we did not speak the language or know anyone there.

So, even though it was not a blessing that a tragedy occurred, it was a blessing that we were not there.

There are so many times in my life when I was in the right place at the right time and NOT at the wrong place at the wrong time. This is called SYNCHRONICITY.

Once, I had a dream that my car was on fire, and a voice in my head said, "Keep driving." That same week, I was driving in San Diego, in the middle lane, at night. A large truck on my left side, the fast lane, suddenly swerved into the center divider, flipped and crashed. There was smoke everywhere. Most people would have hit the brakes from fear, thus causing a bigger accident by getting hit from behind.

My dream said, "Keep driving." So, I did. I was so scared, my hands were shaking, but I drove straight ahead. The other car, once it hit the center divider, was knocked back into my lane, and it missed me by one or two inches. If I had stopped, it would have hit me, and I might have died. Because I kept going, both my car and I were unscathed.

There are so many stories I could write here about divine timing, premonitions, and not being hurt because a little voice or a guardian angel nudged me to go the other way.

It is important to recognize and follow your internal GPS.

How many people were late to work or called in sick on the day of the Twin Towers' attack? I personally know two people who were supposed to be there that day but for synchronistic reasons were not.

While it is annoying when we get stuck behind someone going slowly, or we see a detour sign, or our flight gets cancelled or delayed, remember that maybe a protective miracle is happening in your life.

Two years ago, regrettably, I suffered a miscarriage in the first trimester. I cried and grieved intensely. As disheartening as it was, I did not give up. I trust that the universe has a bigger plan in store for me. What if that baby was not healthy? At the time I got pregnant, I was under a great deal of stress, still grieving the loss of my beloved father. Maybe my body was not strong enough then to carry the baby full-term.

Miscarriages are horrible. Please be especially kind and gentle with anyone you know who has had one. After the loss, I prayed and asked the universe why. The answer I received was profound.

I spoke to a psychic medium named Christine Nightingale who channels the spirits of babies who are in heaven. (2) I wrote her a list of all the questions and concerns I had, and she channeled my baby's answers and sent them back to me. Upon reading my spirit baby's response, I cried —deep, heaving sobs. And I felt relief. She told me that the soul of my baby was never harmed. And that this soul is simply waiting until there is a better opportunity for a stronger body to come into existence. She or he will return to me at the perfect time.

It gave me hope and solace to know this. And it also gives me great hope and encouragement that all of my friends who have lost babies early or later in their pregnancies have beautiful healthy children now. The fact that I got pregnant naturally at forty-eight also gave me hope. It showed me that it was possible. And if it is possible for me, it is possible for others.

In the previous chapter, I wrote about stopovers. Not getting what we want if the timing is not right is divine intervention. When we get to the end of our lives or the afterlife, I believe there will be a flash where we will be able to connect all the dots. We will be able to see how some things fell apart so that better things could fall together.

If you have suffered a loss, I am so sorry. It hurts. Take your time, grieve your pain, cry it out, be with supportive people, or spend time alone if that nurtures you more. Do what you need to do to heal.

I hope you won't lose hope.

Reflection Questions

1. What have you lost that you really wanted? Think back to a time in your life when you lost a loved one. Did you grieve that loss all the way through? Or did you stifle or cover up your grief? Take some time now to write out how you felt/feel. Write a letter to someone you lost, and ask yourself what he or she would say in return.

2. Do you believe that each of us has a soul before we enter our human body? If yes, when do you believe that soul enters the body? And where do you think it goes when we die? There are no right or wrong answers here. I would just like you to reflect upon it and write down what comes to you.

3. For those of you who have been pregnant or are trying to get pregnant, would you be willing to talk to or connect with your future or past children? Would you be willing to try some alternative methods to help you get pregnant? I will include a list of healers I recommend in the index.

4. Have you ever missed a flight, bus, or connection, only to find out that it was a blessing in disguise? What are some of the ways you have experienced a protection miracle? Do you believe we all have a destined time for when we will die? Some people think that is random, and some people think it is decided beforehand. What are your thoughts on this?

5. If it is true that we each have a soul and that soul waits for the perfect opportunity to be born, why do you think you chose to come now? What do you think you were destined to accomplish?

Get Into Action

Make a timeline of your life. On it, include the things that you missed and see if something better came along after. Remember, your life is not over yet, so there are still miracles and opportunities ahead that you can't see yet. Looking at the timeline, do you see how sometimes, what you thought you wanted might not have been as good as what you got later?

Write in your journal all the ways you have been protected by Avoidance Miracles in your life so far.

CHAPTER 44

Austria

LESSON:

Overcoming Fear

The year was 1991. I had recently moved to Milan for graduate school. My boyfriend lived in Trento, which is in Alto Adige/ Südtirol, the northernmost province of Italy. It's a beautiful town nestled in the Alps, not far from the Austrian border.

That winter, we decided to go up to Austria to ski. For my boyfriend and his friends, skiing was something they considered normal and easy because they had all skied since childhood. I grew up in sunny Southern California and had only been skiing once in my life. I was excited but also a little nervous.

When we arrived, the view from the top of the Alps was

magnificent—pure, white snow; bright, blue sky; clear, cold air; and mountain peaks as far as the eye could see. I was in AWE! I felt like I was on the top of the world. It was exhilarating.

If you have ever been skiing, you know that each slope on the mountain is marked by a flag to denote its difficulty. Of course, my group of skiers-since-birth happily took the lift to the triple diamond run, with the black flag aka the most advanced trail. I had only skied on the beginner's runs up to that point. I got to the top of the mountain with them and looked down. Sheer terror. It was steep, rocky, and icy.

I went down the first part crying because I was so scared. They shouted, "C'mon, it's easy!" Yeah, easy for them! In my head, I was cursing them in another language.

They teased me for being too sensitive. "Sei troppo permalosa," they said. It's interesting to note that most of them had spent very little time out of their comfort zones, so they had no idea how it felt to be in my shoes.

It is one thing to be a little nervous to meet your boyfriend's friends, who all speak a different language than you. It's another thing to be a beginning skier on a triple black flag run. One fall and I could break my legs—or worse. I was petrified!

I don't remember how I got down to the bottom. Thank god for my guardian angels who saved me that day. Once I got to the bottom, I headed straight to the lodge and had something hot to drink. Then I bid them all adieu and went off to ski on the easy bunny slopes at my own pace.

There are two great lessons here.

One is about compassion. I saw this so much as a teacher. Just because something is easy for you does not mean it is easy for someone else. Each person is fighting his or her own battle. When my students giggled or mocked a student who was scared to give a presentation, the mama bear in me came out to roar. I know what it feels like to be petrified, and telling someone, "It's easy," is not helpful at all.

The second lesson is that I did make it down that hill. As scared as I was, I made it. It may have taken me longer than everyone else, but I did it.

Looking back at my life, I see how many scary or difficult things I have overcome. And each time, it made me braver. If I can get down a triple black diamond slope in the Austrian Alps, lots of other things pale in comparison.

We must take risks to grow, but there is no one with a timer, rating us on how fast or slow we are. In writing this book and sharing my story, I had to overcome my fears—fear of telling the truth, fear of hurting someone, fear of being judged, etc. There is a reason that not everyone writes a memoir. It takes courage.

The one thing that got me to the end of this book is knowing that I was not writing it for me. I wrote it to help others have the courage to confront their own "black flag slope". We are all inter-connected, so my courage has a ripple effect.

So, whatever that thing is that scares you, take a baby step toward it, even if you have to snow plow all the way down the hill. You will get there eventually, if you just keep taking one step at a time.

Reflection Questions

1. When have you been really scared? Did you face the fear or avoid it? How do you feel about that incident now? Do you wish you had done it differently? If so, how would you do it if you could do it again?

2. Have you ever done something scary or dangerous just to fit in or be cool? Was doing it helpful or harmful to you?

3. What does it mean to be too sensitive? Is it a good thing or a bad thing? Or both? What have you been teased about? Does it still bother you now?

4. Have you ever tried to learn something new as an adult, like a new sport? Did you feel awkward and frightened? Did you keep at it until you became proficient? Did you give up? Why?

Get Into Action

Take a class to learn a new sport, such as tennis, volleyball, salsa dancing, etc. Start in the beginner class. Take ten classes, if possible. Write down how you feel in the first and last class. Confidence is a learned skill. It is like a muscle and needs to be worked out. You will benefit your mind and your body by doing this. Remember, everyone is a beginner in your class, so they will empathize with you if you feel scared or awkward. Go for it!

CHAPTER 45

India

LESSON:

The Healing Power of Yoga

My first experience with Indian spirituality began in 1999, while taking Hatha yoga classes in Los Angeles. I was teaching high school and suffered from constant, severe pain in my neck and upper back. When I went to the doctor, she prescribed muscle relaxants.

When I looked up the long-term effects of prescription medicine, I said, "No, thank you. There must be another way." A friend recommended that I try yoga. The gentle stretching practice of Hatha yoga and meditation eased my pain, so I did not need to take any pain killers.

Although I have not been to India yet, I have visited two Indian ashrams. In 2015, I drove to New Mexico to visit the beautiful Neem Karoli Baba ashram in Taos, New Mexico, founded by Guru Ram Dass, and the magical Babaji Ashram in Crestone, Colorado. Both are free and open to the public. Staying at an ashram is a wonderful way to meditate/chant in community and practice Seva, or sacred service.

I have learned that when my mind is still, my body functions better, my life runs more smoothly, and I do not react to upsetting circumstances the way I used to. By stilling my mind, I am more able to hear the quiet voice within, which is connected to the Divine.

My goddaughter, Cami, is also trained as a Kundalini yoga teacher. We often practice meditation, chant, and sound healing together. The benefits of this practice for her and for me have been life-changing.

Over the years, I have been exposed to many forms of yoga. It is very popular here in California. Paramahansa Yogananda brought yoga to California in 1920, and he created the Self-Realization Fellowship, which I attend regularly. (1)

This past year, I started playing my first crystal sound bowls and the shruti box, an instrument used in chanting of the yoga seed syllables. What I have gained from my many years of studying the Bagavagita, meditation, sound healing, and yoga is a powerful sense of internal peace.

In 2018, I learned a new form of yoga called Yoga of the Voice, developed by Silvia Nakkach. (2) This yoga practice incorporates the power of mantra, music, and chant to heal the body. It is profoundly effective.

While at an intensive workshop of Yoga of the Voice last February, so many memories of my childhood trauma came up to be healed. Every time I had stifled my pain, voice, or anger, that energy got stuck in my throat. When I was young, I sang almost every day. I loved singing. But when I was twelve years old, I stopped. Bullies at school and trauma at home caused me to close my throat chakra. Yoga helped me open that chakra again.

I could not write or publish this book or share all these memories if I had not healed myself. The throat chakra is the energy center which allows us to speak our truth. When it is open and balanced, we feel free to express ourselves. However, if it is closed or imbalanced, we either talk too much or too little.

How many times have I worked with students who were afraid to raise their hand and speak up in class or in front of a group? Thousands of times. So many people have been told to shut up or shut down. How many children who have witnessed or felt abuse in their homes have shut down their voice for fear of being punished? Thousands.

I wrote this book so that I could contribute to the healing on this planet. There are many ways to heal, and yoga is one of them. Yoga is not a physical practice, although in the West, many people think it is. It is a spiritual practice, where you listen to your body. You get still enough to hear what it is saying.

Some cities in the U.S.A. have started using yoga in prisons and at schools. The data shows that the participants are calmer, more collaborative, and have improved health. (3) The health benefits of doing yoga include lower blood pressure, lower cholesterol, stronger muscles, more focus, higher sense of inner peace and well-being, and so on. (4)

There are many ways and forms of practicing yoga. I
encourage everyone to try it. You do not need to fly to India;
you can probably find a yoga center in your city.

Reflection Questions

1. Have you ever tried yoga? Would you be willing to try it? Why or why not?

2. Do you sing? Did you used to sing as a child? Why did you stop? Do you think you are good singer? Why or why not?

3. Are you afraid of speaking in public or in a group? Why? Did you have a traumatic experience in school or at home which may have caused or exacerbated this fear? Write down the details.

4. Have you ever been to an ashram or a kirtan? Or read The Autobiography of a Yogi by Paramahansa Yogananda? What do you think a yogi is? Do you think we need others to teach us about spirituality? What are your thoughts about non-traditional spiritual practices?

5. If you are a parent, have you taught yoga or meditation to your children? What were the results? Do you think your family would benefit from doing some kind of meditation practice together?

Get Into Action

Go to a yoga studio alone or with a family member or friend. Take at least three or more classes before deciding how you feel about it. If you choose yoga, start with something easy and basic like Hatha yoga.

Dedicate ten minutes or more a day to a meditation or chant practice. I personally like to listen to Snatam Kaur. You can find her music on YouTube or iTunes.

Keep a log in your journal on what changes you notice in your body because of your yoga/meditation/chant practice. How does it affect your mood or your relationships?

Book/Movie Recommendation: Eat Pray Love by Elizabeth Gilbert is one of my all-time favorite books/movies. Her writings about India are insightful, comical, and inspirational.

CHAPTER 46

Belgium

LESSON:

Fun in Unexpected Places

On my visit to Holland in 2003, described in Chapter 26, a friend, Marleen, invited me to come and visit her. She lives right on the border between Holland and Belgium. She and her husband came to pick Jose'* and I up and drove us to the city of Ghent in Belgium for the day. Oh, what a blast we had!

Ghent is a city that has retained much of its old European charm. The weather was misty and rainy, and the buildings were ornate and beautiful. Being there truly felt like going back in time.

Marleen wanted to show us this special place that had been built in the 1400s. We walked around the city center for a bit, then happened upon an old building that looked nondescript and went through a small door. It looked like a cave inside. It was a tiny room of about twenty square feet, packed with very jovial folks.

The owner of the establishment welcomed us warmly and spoke Flemish. I did not understand what he was saying, but he looked like such a happy fellow that I just smiled and nodded my head. He brought us these small flutes of liquid in all sorts of magical colors. They were a type of schnapps liquor, a local specialty. The drinks, which looked deceptively harmless, were very strong, and we all proceeded to get very tipsy.

The memories of that day are a little hazy, but I do recall laughing so hard my cheeks hurt and devouring the most amazing Belgian waffles with chocolate sauce. Even though this story is short, the lesson is clear. Fun can be found in the most unexpected places. Be open. Be curious. And one more rule of thumb: any place that is popular with the local people is definitely a place to try.

When I travel, I do not set an agenda. I just ask the locals where they eat and follow the signs. I call it following my internal GPS of synchronicity. Traveling has taught me so many wonderful things and introduced me to so many wonderful people.

Reflection Questions

1. Think about a place you know that looks rather plain on the outside but is a hidden jewel on the inside. Where is it? How did you find it?

2. Think about a person you know who looks plain on the outside but has a wonderful heart and whose company you enjoy a lot. What are the qualities that person exudes which make you feel so good?

3. Have you ever been to a place that is very fancy or expensive and been treated rudely by the staff? Or been disappointed by the quality of the service or food? Where have you been that is pricey but is worth every penny? Which establishments do you believe have excellent service? In what ways do the staff act which makes you feel welcomed?

Get Into Action

Become a tourist in your own city. Explore places you've never been. Go to restaurants you've never tried. Order food you've never eaten. Get out of your comfort zone. Ask locals in other neighborhoods where they eat. Go there. Write about your experience. What did you discover?

SIDE-NOTE

I recently discovered the most wonderful teahouse in San Juan Capistrano, CA. I had driven by that town perhaps a thousand times while driving from Los Angeles to San Diego. My husband happened to discover this teahouse one day when we got lost. You never know what magical places you might find. Get lost in your own city and see what happens.

CHAPTER 47

USA: The North Pole, Alaska

LESSON:

Keep a Dream Journal

In 2002, I was working in Seoul, South Korea as an English teacher after taking one year off to travel around the world. I knew it was time for me to go back to the United States, but I was not sure where I wanted to live. I did not want to go back to Los Angeles, so I made a list of potential cities, which included San Diego, Sedona, and Santa Fe.

I had been keeping a dream journal for many years. I learned to write down a question before going to sleep, and the answers would come to me in my dreams. I used Carl Yung's book of dream symbols to interpret the meaning of my dreams.

I asked my subconscious which city would be the best next place for me to move to. And, always, the answer came. I kept having dreams of jewels, sapphires, diamonds, and rubies. They would be on my clothes, or I would find them in box. One day, it occurred to me. Jewels. The Jewel. La Jolla, a beautiful part of San Diego, pronounced "Hoya", sounds like the word for jewel in Spanish, la joya.

Another second sign of confirmation came when I realized that the three books I was reading at the time were all penned by authors who lived in San Diego: Deepak Chopra, Louise Hay, and Tony Robbins. That confirmed it for me. I said to myself, "If these three leaders have chosen San Diego as their home, then there must be some good energy there!"

In September of 2003, I moved to San Diego. I had one good friend, my college roommate, who lived there. So, I rented a tiny house near where she lived in North Park. On the day I moved in, the landlord and her friend were sitting outside in the garden we shared. Her friend said "hello" and asked me what I did as my profession.

I replied, "I am a teacher, but I am here in San Diego to attend Grossmont College to become a professional photographer."

She said, "Oh! You must go to this event tonight here in North Park. It is called Ray at Night, on Ray St. It is a big art event with live music."

So, I went. I walked around all the galleries in my new city and thought to myself, one day, I will have my own art show here. That was in 2003.

I finished photography school in 2005, started my own company called Miraclecatcher Photography, and taught part-time at UCSD. All the while, I wrote daily in my dream journal.

One morning, in 2007, I woke up from a dream and thought, I have to go to the North Pole! Many of you would laugh this thought off, but if you have come this far in the book, you know that I do not take messages from the universe lightly. I got a map out and located North Pole, Alaska, which just so happens to be where Santa Claus Village is located.

As a teacher at university, I had vacation breaks every quarter, which worked well with my traveling and photography. So, I booked a flight to Anchorage. I had always wanted to go to Alaska. For someone who loves nature and nature photography, it is an absolute dream come true.

I went to Alaska in June 2007 and spent three weeks there. I rented a car and drove fifteen hundred miles from Anchorage, down to Homer, and up to Fairbanks, to stop at North Pole.

I brought two cameras and two lenses. I rented a car because there were so many wonderful stops to make. There were moose on the side of the road, views of Mount Denali (McKinley) peeking through the clouds, boat trips to see the orcas, and salmon jumping up the rivers. Wow. Alaska, like New Zealand, is mostly uninhabited and feels like a slice of heaven.

I took some of the best photos of my career on that trip. And I even got to whisper my Christmas wish in Santa's ear at Santa's Village--a dream which later came true.

When I got back from Alaska in July, I went to Ray at Night in San Diego to see the art shows. I walked into one gallery and started chatting with the owner. I told him about my recent trip to Alaska. He got an excited look on his face and said, "Can you do an art show here in September? I have another artist who doing a show of work from Antarctica. Your pieces would be perfect to show with his!"

And just like divine timing always works so miraculously, my first big art show opened a few days after my fortieth birthday.

Wishes do come true.

So, you see, if I had not followed my dream messages, I would have never gone to San Diego or Alaska. Each message takes you to the next step.

Synchronistically, that same year, in 2007, one of my photography clients hired me to design a new upscale line of... guess what? Jewelry. And guess where he lived? In La Jolla.

You just can't make this stuff up. It really does work!

(P. S. Although Alaska is not a country now, up until 1867, it was part of Russia. (1) And Santa's Village is definitely worth a visit. It is a little country of its own.)

Reflection Questions

1. Do you remember your dreams? Do you write them down?
   Have you ever asked questions and gotten the answer in
   your dreams? Do you have one recurring dream? Have you
   investigated what the possible meaning is? What do you
   think it means?

2. Have you ever received a message or hunch that you followed
   up on? What was the result? Have you ever not followed a
   hunch? What was the result of that decision?

3. Did you ever ask for something and then later met someone
   who offered you the very thing you asked for? Think about
   it and write it down. Anything counts, even if it was a small
   thing.

4. Do you feel like it might be time to change your living situation, city, or profession? How will you determine where to go next? Are you willing to ask your subconscious mind for an answer by using a dream journal? If so, follow the action step below.

Get Into Action

Get a notebook. Put it beside your bedside table. Set your alarm clock ten minutes earlier than you normally wake up. (This is important because it makes it easier to remember your dreams.) Before going to sleep, write down one question in the journal, for example, where should I move to? Or which company or school should I apply to?

Every day for thirty days, write down everything you remember from your dreams. Look for patterns and symbols. Google "dream symbols" or read Carl Jung's book on dreams. Pay attention to signs during your waking hours too. Do this consistently for thirty days, and you will get an answer. You need to be open-minded about this answer. It may not be the answer you were expecting.

CHAPTER 48

Taiwan

LESSON:

Conviction

In 1995, I landed in Taiwan on a stopover to Hong Kong. I did not stay very long. However, I have taught many Taiwanese students over the course of my career, and I believe that the history of Taiwan demonstrates a powerful lesson for us all.

Taiwan's story is a classic tale of triumph over great odds. In 1949, the Chinese followers of Chiang Kai-Shek fled the mainland of China during the Communist Revolution. They fled to a small island in the South China Sea, called Taiwan. With a population of only circa seven million people in 1949, that small island nation has not only survived in the shadow of its much larger neighbor, it has prospered. (1)

Like several other countries I have written about in this book, size does not matter when it comes to success. In fact, there are so many nations that are much larger than Taiwan, with many more natural resources, which are not nearly as successful.

Taiwan has thrived for over fifty years, in spite of the fact that there have been numerous threats of invasion. I believe that conviction is a powerful force to be reckoned with. One person defending his or her home is stronger than ten or even one hundred hired soldiers. The families who fled to Taiwan in 1949 had conviction, and they have instilled that value into their society. Apathy is the opposite of conviction. Apathy is the disease of not caring about anything. In many Western countries, we can see how the disease of apathy has taken its toll on the political and educational systems.

Recently, while at a conference on Buddhism, I learned about a female Buddhist monk named Cheng Yen, who started the Tzu Chi Foundation and built several schools and free hospitals in Taiwan. She is one of my new heroes. The staff of the schools and hospitals works mostly on a voluntary basis. Her schools teach nutrition, recycling, philanthropy, and holistic health practices, which are a model from which we could all learn. Her foundation has been so successful, in fact, that it has sent millions of dollars in foreign aid to many countries across the globe. (2)

If one woman with a weak heart in Taiwan can raise millions of dollars in foreign aid and create a global charity with over ten million members, what could we all do if we had more conviction? What would happen if we all stood up to our inner and outer demons? How would the world change for the better if we all chose to have that kind of conviction?

I wonder...

Reflection Questions

1. Were you ever intimidated by someone bigger, stronger, or older than you? When? What did they do or say to threaten you? Did you confront that person? Did you avoid them? How does that experience still affect you today?

2. Where in your life are you apathetic? Cynical? Giving up? Journal on this until you can find the root of when you stopped trying or caring. What action could you take now to be more proactive and renew your passion?

Get Into Action

Choose something in your life which you used to love but somehow lost interest in. For example, did you used to play an instrument or feel passionately about a specific cause? Commit to renewing your passion in this area. Sign up for a class or volunteer to stand up for a cause you believe in.

Conviction is like a muscle. It needs to be used.

Choose one person in your life who you need to stand up to. Who is that person? What do you need to say to them? Be proactive in your communication. Tell them how you feel. If you do not speak up for yourself, no one will do it for you.

CHAPTER 49

Yugoslavia

LESSON:

Timing is Everything

The year was 1996. I was in a long-distance relationship with a man named Dario* from Trieste, which is on the border between Italy and Slovenia. His father was Italian and his mother Slovenian. At that time, Slovenia was still part of Yugoslavia.

We had met in Thailand the year before. When we met, everything seemed perfect. Like many vacation romances, everything was so easy and relaxed. However, after several weeks on the idyllic islands of Koh Tao and Koh Phangan, we both had to go back to our "real world" lives. Dario worked at his family's hotel and was about to start his one year obligatory military service in Italy. I was about to begin graduate school in

NYC, something I had been dreaming of for a long time.

Dario was kind and loyal and younger than me. He vowed to love and cherish me and asked me to wait for him to finish his military service. He wrote beautiful love letters. I would fly to visit him when he had time off, and we would travel the Italian countryside and go into Slovenia to visit the wineries and the casino. I met his parents, who were lovely, and all three of them flew over to America to meet me for Christmas.

At the time, I was pursuing my Master's degree to become a university professor. I did not want to live in a small town or run a family business. Not that there is anything wrong with those things; but I was twenty-seven years old, I lived in New York City, and had my whole future ahead of me. Needless to say, I was not ready to settle down. So our relationship fizzled.

Two years later, I had returned to Los Angeles and started teaching. I was going on dates, but the men I was meeting were superficial and non-committal. I thought nostalgically about the sweet Italian/Slovenian boy who was so romantic.

Life always has a funny way of bringing us back in a spiral. You meet the same people at a different time with a different perspective.

So, I wrote to him.

They say hindsight has fifty-fifty vision. Maybe. Maybe not. We were older. He had finished his military service and was now working full-time. I was more mature and looking for someone serious. I thought, maybe it could work this time...

So, off I flew to meet him in Venice. Sounds romantic, doesn't it? Well, it was. I found him more mature and even more handsome. It was a potent combination, and he was much more solid than the men I had been meeting in my city. Our reunion went splendidly, and I started playing out scenarios in my head of moving back to Italy to live with him.

However, the dynamic had changed. I was more interested now. I was more available. He had just gone through a terrible break-up and was not ready to commit his heart fully. The man who had written letters of undying love, who had followed me across several continents, was now unsure, indecisive, and scared.

Had he changed? Yes. Had I? Yes.

I have heard it said that timing is everything, and yes, timing is very important. In order for love to flourish, both partners must be ready for commitment at the same time.

I think Dario is married now. He still lives in that same small town and runs his family business. I wish him well.

When it comes to manifestation, it is very important that we be 100% ready and aligned for what we ask for. It is also important to consider the free will of the other parties involved.

Now, at fifty, when I make a request to the Universal Bank in the Sky, I ask for a specific outcome or "something better".

Sometimes, what we want is not in the highest good of all persons involved.

When it comes to marriage, babies, corporate mergers, or partnerships of any kind, it takes two to tango. Sometimes, you are doing everything right and are fully aligned with what you want, but it still is not happening. Super frustrating, I know. However, what if the other person is not ready?

In previous chapters, I talked about pregnancy. What happens when a woman gets pregnant and her partner is not ready? Usually, a lot of fighting and possibly separation. At best, the couple might stay together but in a very lonely marriage. The children and both parents usually suffer.

If someone is not ready, let them go. Letting go and surrendering is the most powerful way to shift energy. Sometimes, all it takes for the other person to get ready is to simply back off and let them decide on their own.

It takes trust to surrender. Trust that the timing will get better, or that a better opportunity will present itself.

Looking back, those many years ago with Dario, I would do it all the same way again. Why? Because it was fun, romantic, and adventurous. And it was a stopover on my journey to marriage. Many years later, I would meet a wonderful man from a small town who used to work in his family business. I would meet him in my city, not a million miles away. And the best part is, we would both be ready.

Reflection Questions

1. Did you ever meet the right person at the wrong time? Reflect on this. What was the gift of this relationship? What did you learn?

2. Did you ever get a great opportunity, but it came at a time you were not ready for it? What was the opportunity? Did you take it or not? Why or why not

3. What do you need to let go of right now? Where are youpushing to make something happen, or for someone to do what you want? What happens when you back off?

4. Nostalgia is tricky. It sometimes makes people look better than they actually are. Write about someone you broke up with or who broke up with you, and you got back together because of nostalgia. How did that work out? Better or worse? Were the reasons you broke up in the first place still present?

5. Did you ever meet someone on vacation who seemed great until you got back home? Why are vacation romances so great? How do you act differently when you are on vacation in a foreign place? Are you less inhibited? Why do we change when we get home? What are some ways we could bring that feeling of vacation romance home with us and keep it going back home?

Get Into Action

Go to Google or Facebook and look up someone you used to date when you were young. How are they different now? How are you different now? You do not need to contact them directly. Just observe. Would you have been happy with them now? What surprises you about them now? Look at old photos of yourself when you were in high school. How have you changed? Have you improved or let yourself go? Pick one trait that you used to have that you liked and start incorporating more of it into your personality now. Journal what shifts you see.

CHAPTER 50

Argentina

LESSON:

Connecting the Dots

As I come to the final chapter in this book, I am beginning a new chapter in my life. Without a doubt, there will be more stories to share and a new book to write.

In August 2015, my life changed drastically. Over the course of 30 days, I retired from teaching after over twenty-five years and left the city I had been living in for twelve years. I moved back into my father's house to care for him 24/7 in hospice and held him in my arms as his soul left his body.

Every day, while I was nursing my father, I would take a break and go to the beach near his house. It soothed my soul just to stare at the ocean and listen to the waves. Near that beach, I often stopped at a little Mexican restaurant to eat. On the day he died, after they took the body away, I had to get outside and breathe. The air in the house was stifling. I was physically and mentally exhausted and very hungry. So, my dad's wife and I stopped in that little Mexican cafe to get some food to go. Then, we sat and watched the sunset, had a good cry, and said goodbye to our favorite person.

Sorting through the mountains of paperwork after his passing and running the family business was so overwhelming that all I could do was just get out of bed and do one thing at a time. My advice for anyone who is grieving: just do one thing on your to-do list per day. Sometimes, just getting dressed is that one thing.

Slowly, slowly—be gentle with yourself.

A few weeks later, I found myself at that same little Mexican café. I knew the waiters well and chatted with them Spanish.

A handsome man with kind eyes came to the table beside me and asked in Spanish if he could sit there. I replied, "Por su puesto." (Of course.)

He asked me where I was from, since I was speaking in Spanish. I told him that I was American, but that I used to live in Spain. He had a different accent, so I asked him where he was from.

"Argentina," he replied.

And so, you see how the last chapter in this book is also the beginning of a new chapter in my life.

The rest, as they say, is history.

On my fiftieth birthday, I married that Argentine man. It was a dream come true for both of us.

The person who had traveled all over the world, looking for love, found it when she was least expecting it. Right there, a few blocks from the street where she grew up as a child.

They say that love comes to us in the most unexpected ways. I am a testament to that. Miracles happen when we let go and let God.

When my father died, my heart broke. It was the saddest and hardest time in my life. But God got in through those cracks in my heart. My father left such a large vacant space in my heart that not one, but two, loves showed up: my beloved husband and my beautiful stepson. And together, they filled my heart, which now overflows with love again.

Thank you Papi for sending them to me.

When I look back through these chapters, at all the journeys I took and people I met, I see clearly how our lives DO make sense. There are dots and they do connect, as Steve Jobs so eloquently explained in his commencement speech at Stanford University. (1)

Why did I study Spanish and live in Spain? Why was I in Los Angeles on that day, at that time, instead of in another city? Why did my father choose to exit his body on that day, not before or later? Why was I always attracted to men who were from other countries? Why did I not get married sooner? Why did I go to that restaurant on that day?

Why? Why? Why?

Because all of those moments led me to this moment now.

I believe that the mistakes I made were blessings in disguise. I believe I am meant to be exactly where I am now. I believe that all of our lives are a giant chess game, in which all the lessons are interconnected.

Now I have a new last name: Olivera, which comes from the olive tree. Olive trees have always been a symbol of peace.

After fifty years of learning these lessons, I have climbed my mountain, vanquished my demons, and found happiness.

I hope this book has opened up new possibilities for you and made you realize the gifts in your life by connecting the dots. I hope that by answering the reflection questions and taking the action steps, you are experiencing new miracles in your life.

At the very least, I hope this book has inspired you to see the world for yourself and live new and interesting adventures.

Above all, I hope this book has given you hope.

For with hope, all things are possible.

Deep breaths and heart hugs,

Micaela Miraclecatcher xo

AFTERWORD

Today is September 29th, 2018. It is Michelmas, or St. Michael's Day. A little over one year ago, I started writing this book. How apropos it is that I complete the final page on this day. Archangel Michael is the bringer of light, he who dispels fear and vanquishes darkness. By sharing his name, I was given the same life purpose.

As I sit writing, a miracle baby is growing in my womb, a most beautiful being of light. He, too, will be named after an angel, just as my father and I were. If you have read through this book, you will understand why I waited until the very end to share this surprising and joyous news with you.

I wrote this book for those of you who feel like giving up. There were so many times when I too felt like giving up and questioned my faith in a higher power. However, after so many years of praying and struggling and defeating my own demons, I can definitely say it was all worth it.

There is a passage in the Bible which says, "So I will restore to you the years that the locust has eaten (Joel 2:25). I finally understand what this phrase means. My life has been a vivid example of how the greatest gifts come to those who persevere though the darkness. Now, at age fifty-one, I feel stronger, healthier, and more fertile than I have ever felt.

In the foreword, I said that this book was more of a handbook than an autobiography. If you have been following along with the reflection questions and taking those action steps, you will no doubt feel and see a difference in your life. If you skipped parts, go back. Do them again. There is no way to avoid life's tests, but we can confront them with grace.

It is the fight that makes us stronger. It is the sweetness of the reward that makes us appreciate the gift, and it is through the journey that happiness is found.

For you, dear readers, I wish you love, courage, and strength. Go forth, like archangel Michael with your swords of light, and conquer those fears. Do not give into the darkness. May abundance, joy, and miracles surround you and shower down upon you.

Until we meet again,

MM

Final Reflection Questions

1. What is the most important thing you learned from this book?

2. What changes have you noticed in your life since you started taking the action steps?

3. What is something you learned about yourself that surprised you?

4. What is something you always wanted to try, and now because of this book you will?

5. Is there an area where you were feeling stuck before and now you feel empowered?

6. Who do you know that would benefit from reading this book?

7. Do you view people differently now than you did before you started reading this book?

8. Which chapters did you find the most challenging to read? What resistance came up for you? Were you able to move past it?

9. What is one area in your life where you had given up hope or felt cynical and you now have new inspiration or motivation?

10. Were you able to see how the dots connect in your life? Which lessons were necessary for you to move on the next level?

REFERENCES

Chapter 3:
1. http://zenstudies.org/teachings/what-is-zen/

Chapter 4:
1. https://en.wikipedia.org/wiki/Khmer_Rouge_rule_of_
   Cambodia

Chapter 7:
1. https://www.independent.co.uk/news/world/europe/italy-
   sees-devalued-lira-as-a-defeat-1551508.html

Chapter 10:
1. https://www.sonima.com/fitness/healing-water/
2. https://www.dailymail.co.uk/health/article-102698/Three-
   health-benefits-sea.html
3. http://www.masaru-emoto.net/english/water-crystal.html
4. https://www.edgarcayce.org/the-readings/health-and-
   wellness/holistic-health-database/therapies-epsom-salts-
   baths/

Chapter 12:
1. Hay, L. You Can Heal Your Life (Hay House, 1999)
2. https://blog.mindvalley.com/7chakras/?utm_
   source=google_blog

Chapter 13:
1. https://www.thoughtco.com/twin-telepathy-best-
   evidence-2593932
2. https://mctfr.psych.umn.edu/research/UM%20research.html
3. http://mentalfloss.com/article/60632/11-scientific-reasons-
   why-being-nature-relaxing

Chapter 18:
1. http://havanajournal.com/politics/entry/a-list-of-what-the-cuban-people-can-not-do-in-cuba/

Chapter 19:
1. https://en.wikipedia.org/wiki/Vatican_City
2. https://www.wakingtimes.com/2017/08/03/much-wealth-vatican/
3. https://money.cnn.com/2015/09/24/news/pope-francis-visit-vatican-catholic-church/index.html

Chapter 20:
1. https://en.wikipedia.org/wiki/Rwandan_Civil_War
2. https://www.consciouslifestylemag.com/cellular-memory-healing-clearing/
3. https://www.medicalnewstoday.com/articles/156285.php

Chapter 22:
1. https://www.history.com/topics/vietnam-war/cu-chi-tunnels

Chapter 24:
1. https://getfitforbirth.com/a-mothers-emotions-affect-her-unborn-child/
2. Lipton, B. The Biology of Belief (Hay House 2005)
3. https://catherinecarrigan.com/seven-generation-healing/
4. https://www.huffingtonpost.com/dr-judith-rich/healing-the-wounds-of-you_b_853632.html
5. https://www.sciencealert.com/scientists-observe-epigenetic-memories-pas
6. https://www.psychologytoday.com/us/blog/matter-personality/201207/why-is-it-so-hard-families-change-repetitive-dysfunctional-patterns
7. https://www.psychologytoday.com/us/blog/evil-deeds/200806/essential-secrets-psychotherapy-repetitive-relationship-patterns

Chapter 28:
1. https://www.businessinsider.com/things-that-are-illegal-in-singapore-2015-7
2. https://tradingeconomics.com/singapore/gdp
3. http://statisticstimes.com/economy/projected-world-gdp-capita-ranking.php
4. https://www.psychologytoday.com/us/blog/the-truisms-wellness/201607/the-powerful-psychology-behind-cleanliness
5. https://thoughtcatalog.com/lana-jane-fox/2013/11/5-reasons-neat-people-are-more-successful/

Chapter 29:
1. https://www.edgarcayce.org/the-readings/health-and-wellness/holistic-health-database/therapies-epsom-salts-baths/
2. https://www.naturallivingideas.com/dead-sea-salt/

Chapter 32:
1. https://en.wikipedia.org/wiki/One-child_policy

Chapter 33:
1. https://visitsedona.com/spiritual-wellness/what-is-a-vortex/
2. https://ascendedrelationships.com/7-signs-that-you-have-cords-of-attachments/

Chapter 34:
1. www.harmoniousearth.org/earths-major-chakra-points-and-vortexes-the-sacred-sites/
2. https://www.glastonburytor.org.uk/makermyths.html

Chapter 36:
1. Hay, L. You Can Heal Your Life (Hay House, 1999)

Chapter 37:
1. The Lion King, Hakuna Matata: https://youtu.be/nbY_aP-alkw

Chapter 38:
1. https://www.to-hawaii.com/hawaiian-myths-and-legends.php
2. https://en.wikipedia.org/wiki/Kingdom_of_Hawaii

Chapter 39:
1. http://www.casinomontecarlo.com/casinos-2/casino-monte-carlo-2/about-casino/
2. http://healthywealthynwise.com/?p=17000
3. https://www.cnbc.com/2017/08/25/heres-why-lottery-winners-go-broke.html
4. https://www.businessinsider.com/winning-powerball-lottery-happiness-2017-8

Chapter 40:
1. https://en.wikipedia.org/wiki/Past_life_regression
2. https://en.wikipedia.org/wiki/Nubia

Chapter 41:
1. https://en.wikipedia.org/wiki/Shenzhen
2. http://letstalknutrition.com/traditional-chinese-medicine-part-i-the-ying-and-yang-of-health/
3. https://www.themindfulword.org/2013/yin-yang/
4. https://en.wikipedia.org/wiki/Li_Ching-Yuen
5. The Story of Li Ching Yuen: "Tortoise-Pigeon-Dog". Time Magazine. 15 May 2012.

Chapter 42:
1. Hicks, Esther and Jerry, Ask and It Is Given (Hay House 2004)